FROM NO CO

Edgar Alan Cole, M.B.A.

A REALISTIC APPROACH TO BUILDING A SIX-FIGURE INCOME AND

REAL EXAMPLES OF HOW IT CAN BE DONE

STOP CHASING MILLION-DOLLAR DREAMS AND GET $100,000 FIRST

ISBN-10: 1463565844
ISBN-13: 978-1463565848

Nashville: One Team Publishing, LLC

DEDICATION

I dedicate this book to my late father, mother, and sister: Rev. James L. Cole, Jr., Eddie Earline Cole, and Arketa Denise Cole. Oh! I didn't forget about you Kim.

ACKNOWLEDGMENTS

Even though writing this book was a long and challenging journey, it was well worth it. I would like to thank the Lord for blessing me with the wisdom and opportunity to complete this project. I would also like to thank my sister, Felicia Armstrong; my brother-in-law, Earlest Armstrong, Jr.; my nephew Earlest Armstrong, III and his beautiful family; my nephew James Daniel Cole; my nephew Cory Armstrong; the Phelps family: Uncle Leon (thank you for being a great inspiration and example of how to be a man), Aunt Ollie, Cousin Harold; all of my family in Lynchburg, TN; the rest of the Cole, Armstrong, Long, Phelps, and Dunnivant families; Ebony Harris (thank you for the great ideas and believing in me); Traci Galbreath for her outstanding editing; my entire One Team family: Todd, Gary, Antawan (88 Keys), Dewandus, and Jamison; my cousin Jeff Phelps for his Georgetown Law advice and believing in the dream from day one; my cousin Ilya for her "life" advice; Reverend Martinas Frazier, Sr. for his spiritual advice; Jay Farrell for the fantastic photos; Mignon and the entire Francois family; Johnny (Tink), Devron (Chubb), Kimberly, Kisha and the entire Jackson family; the rest of my crew: Mike (Wise), James (Jazz), Glen (Manfred), Winston (Ranks), Chip, Johnny (Jinx), Laturel, Judah, Shaun (Asia D), Flip, Thomas, , Kim (my other sister), Mark (my big brother), Angela, Kristin, Carla, Robin, Erica, Donna, Sheneca, Tremaine, Sonya, Melanie, Code Red, Rod and the rest of the Costlofobic crew, Will, T.C. Bryant, and Terrance; my spiritual family: Greater First Street Missionary Baptist Church; Luckett Lodge #137; my fellow alumni of Hunters Lane High School; my fellow alumni of the University of Louisville; my fellow alumni of the University of Phoenix; my fellow Army Veterans; the great cities of Nashville, Louisville, Indianapolis, and Chicago, where I learned how to hustle; and anyone I might have missed. Thank you everyone.

FROM NO COLLAR TO A WHITE COLLAR

Preface: A Dream Must Not Interfere with Reality

Ever since I was a kid I dreamed of being rich, having the biggest house in the neighborhood, and the finest cars. When I finally woke up reality was staring me right in the face. I was 33 years old, recently laid off from a good job, and facing foreclosure on my home. What happened to my dreams? I graduated from college and had landed the dream job. I should have been living the American dream, but I was broke, unemployed, and clueless about what my next move should be. There is nothing wrong with dreaming about wealth as long as you are realistic when you wake up. This was my reality, and I was determined to be successful by any means necessary, as long as I could do it legit. The first thing I had to figure out was where did I go wrong, and why did I lose everything in a blink of an eye? The one thought that continued to run through my mind was the fact that I was dreaming too much and not facing reality. While I was dreaming of being a millionaire, I had never even made $100,000 and had no idea about how to get that type of money. The reason I focused on making a $100,000 is that I had made an average of $50,000 a year for the past five years, and I was still struggling. The capitalistic society we live in today has eliminated the middle class. There are only the "haves" and the "have nots" in our society. I was tired of not having the things I wanted. It was time to raise the stakes in my personal goals, and a six-figure income would definitely give me the financial freedom to do the things that I wanted to do.

If I didn't know how to obtain that type of wealth, the best place to start was scanning my environment for individuals who "had." Some of these individuals were everyday citizens making substantial earnings in unlikely industries. Construction, communications, and cooking were a few. These individuals had crossed my path several times, but I was too busy talking instead of listening. After I realized that these individuals had accomplished what I was trying to achieve, I asked them to tell me their stories about how they made it. One of the individuals had been to prison and is now a millionaire. His prosperity did not come overnight, but he did make $100,000 within four years of being released from prison. If your electricity was scheduled to be cut off and the bank had scheduled a foreclosure on your home, what would you do? Would you throw your hands in the air and scream "I give," or would you trust your faith, move into action, and get that money? The woman I met was facing these challenges and decided to put her faith in God. She started her own business and took her city by storm. When she made these decisions, she went from facing foreclosure on her home to having one of the top bakeries in her city. She did this without borrowing one dime from a bank, and her business is still completely debt free. I used to laugh at door-to-door salesmen, until I met one making six figures by providing a commodity that ultimately sold itself. How could this be possible? While most people, including me, were making excuses for why they were being denied the American dream, these individuals were getting serious money.

The one thing that these individuals had in common was that they stopped making excuses. You may have heard some of these excuses: no one will hire me, I have a criminal record, I don't know how to make money, the system is designed for me to fail, I don't have the education, and the list goes on. An excuse is nothing more than a mental roadblock that we create to hinder our full potential. To be successful you have to recondition your mind to refuse failure and know that anything is possible. Individuals have to own themselves and not be held captive by a dead-end job, unemployment, past mistakes, and pride. Pride keeps us from seeing the bigger picture and makes us focus only on our current situation. The individuals I chose for my case studies saw the bigger picture and took what was theirs, legally and successfully. There are no losers in this book, only winners who focused on long-term success instead of short-term relief.

Some individuals get lucky and hit the lottery for millions, or discover the next big idea. But most individuals end up in a dead-end job working for a boss they despise. This doesn't have to be your future. Your future can be mapped out with short-term goals, strategically developed for long-term objectives. Anybody can make a six-figure income by using a strategy that I like to call "multi-hustling." Hustling is often perceived as an illegal activity that usually involves hurting others or yourself. Anytime I mention hustling in this book, it should be perceived as a legal activity that keeps you out of prison and the grave while accumulating substantial wealth. There is nothing wrong with being a hustler, but there is something wrong with putting your life or someone else's life in danger. Simply put, you must be a legal hustler instead of an illegal one. The individuals I wrote about in this book have peace of mind and sleep well at night. They don't worry about going to jail or losing their lives to the unnecessary violence associated with illegal hustling. I have heard the cliché "don't put all of your eggs in one basket" my entire life, and I always let it go in one ear and out the other. But now I have incorporated it into my concept of multi-hustling. Using this concept, you must have more than one source of income to achieve sustained financial security and a six-figure income.

This is not a get rich quick manifesto or a book of dreams. This is a book based on reality and creating a blueprint for concrete wealth. If you are not willing to leave your pride at the door, work hard, and tap into various sources of knowledge (mostly common sense), you will miss the entire concept of this book. One of the main skills that I developed while conducting my research was learning how to listen. I had to learn how to shut up, listen to others, and soak up every bit of knowledge I could get. Even though I have a master's degree in business administration, I learned how to make money in the streets of knowledge and on the corners of opportunity. The main reason I wrote this book was to inspire others to stop making excuses and chasing million-dollar dreams that were unlikely to come true. When you see those incredible infomercials late at night about making millions and retiring forever, they don't tell you that their money is made when you stop believing in yourself and decide to throw your good money into some useless system designed to make them rich and not you! I wonder how many infomercials they would make if you understood that concept. Why do these infomercials come on so late at night? Because that is the time of night when individuals who are worried about making ends meet and about how to dig themselves out of their current situation can't sleep. I would rather you spend that time discovering your own ideas and opportunities rather than building someone else's wealth. Never view a sleepless night as a burden, but use it as an opportunity to brainstorm on how to get money. Some of the best ideas come in the middle of the night when you can't sleep. That is why I sleep with a pen and pad next to my bed. I have had many sleepless nights and know how it feels. My dreams didn't become a reality until I took control of my sleepless nights and made them benefit me. Now, I sleep well at night because I own myself and treat every experience as an opportunity to learn, regardless whether the experience was good or bad.

Owning yourself doesn't always mean being the owner of the company but being the owner of your situation. Why own the company when you can make the company work for you? It's a simple concept, but individuals often make it harder than it really is. This doesn't mean there is anything wrong with being an entrepreneur, because being the owner of your own business is a wonderful feeling and can be quite rewarding. After reading this book you will know what a real boss is, and you probably have been one all this time but just didn't realize it. I didn't recognize this fact for a long time, but I don't regret it. Regret is for losers and individuals not willing to take risks. You have to be a risk taker to be successful, but the key to taking risks is mitigating failure before it ever occurs. The reason I put so much emphasis on the case studies developed for this book is that failure was substantially reduced by the practices of the individuals studied.

These individuals were so successful because they recognized a need in their environment and simply fulfilled that need. I want you to study real examples and techniques on how to recognize a need in your environment and capitalize on it. Before you can capitalize on that need, I want you to first capitalize on yourself. This book is designed for you to immediately invest in yourself by the time you are finished with the last page. Investing in yourself doesn't always require money, but it does require your time and making the best of it. The concept of going from having no collar to a white collar is literally and symbolically wearing the uniform of an executive. Executives and entrepreneurs wear a white collar as a symbol of his or her status in the hierarchy of this capitalistic society. You have been left out of the board room and the owner's box for far too long. It is time for you to wear the white collar. You will be able to own the company when the company will still think it owns you.

Even though your journey will not always be easy, you should be glad that it is not. Trials and tribulations should be viewed as challenges of your inner strengths and ambitions instead of a barrel of burdens. I have often heard that what doesn't kill a person only makes him or her stronger. If this is this case, why not go all out with the one life you have to live? This means that it is never too late to accomplish your dreams, as long as they are pursued with realistic goals and the right approach. This also means that it is never too early to start planning ahead for the things you want in life regardless of your current situation.

After reading this book you should be able to dismiss every excuse for being unsuccessful. If an ex-convict can do it, why can't you? If a mother of six can do it, why can't you? If an unemployed veteran in the midst of a terrible recession can do it, why can't you? I know that you can be successful with a different approach and a more productive way of thinking. The one thing I can't do is make decisions for you, but I can give you guidance on how to make better ones. Even though I have been very successful in my own ventures, I started by listening to others who had what I wanted in life and learned how they did it. That is why I am sharing their concepts as well as mine. You will get to where you want to be as long as you don't quit. Anytime I have ever thought about quitting, I think about the race not going to the swift but to the one who endures to the end. Now, it's time to get money with a realistic approach.

PART I

THE FOUNDATION

I OWN YOURSELF

The first questions you should ask yourself are, "who am I?" and "what am I worth?" Most individuals are either the owner or the worker. As workers, most individuals believe their worth is minimal compared to the worth of the company. This is far from the truth. Workers are the heartbeat of the company but fail to realize it. Even though being the heartbeat of an organization sounds good, it's still the wrong way to view yourself. Stop viewing yourself as an employee and stop viewing the company you work for as an employer. Instead you should look at yourself as a corporation and your employer as a customer.

SOLD!

For example, the name of my corporation is Edgar Alan Cole. The Edgar Alan Cole Corporation has over 15 years of experience in business management and leading companies in the right direction with outstanding leadership, technical expertise, and knowledge. That is just one example of how you can completely control your situation at all times, in your mind, which translates into reality. In my mind, I refuse to ever work for another individual, and I vow to always be the boss! If you are unemployed, you still are a corporation who presents his or her business plan (your job resume) to potential customers (also known as employers) for the purpose of improving their organizations. Why is it so important to understand this concept? The main reason is that businesses try to meet or exceed the expectations of their customers.

If you always view yourself as a corporation and your employer as a customer, then you are more likely to remove yourself from organizational politics and focus on making money. Too often, I would get a good job and get caught up in organizational politics. I was worried about the boss not liking me and which co-workers were talking about me instead of making money. After I adopted the concept of being my own boss, I wasn't worried about making friends on the job or the boss liking me. My performance would speak for itself. My focus was meeting or exceeding the expectations of the customer and making as much money as I could.

Your worth can be determined by which skills, education, and technical expertise you possess. A self examination of your worth will help you determine what direction you would like to go with your long-term goals. If you are lacking the skills, education, and technical expertise that customers are seeking, then it is time to acquire the tools customers would like you to have. Another key factor in determining worth is identifying your assets and liabilities. Assets are the things you own such as disposable income, savings, investments, home equity, and property.

Liabilities are the things you owe such as loans, living expenses, mortgage payments, and car payments. The ultimate goal is to have a balance between assets and liabilities to stabilize your financial situation. Companies use balance sheets to stabilize assets and liabilities. If you are just starting to determine your financial worth, simply writing down your assets and liabilities is a good place to start. Remember, if you don't own it, it's not yours. Ownership is a critical factor in creating wealth. I began my quest for financial independence with $10,000 worth of equity in my home and $60,000 worth of debt. In other words, I was way out of balance. Even though I was seriously in debt, knowledge of my situation immediately gave me ownership.

I knew who I was, financially, and I had to make a change. Considering myself as a corporation and my employer as a customer, I lost my only form of income when my customer decided to lay me off. This was a serious reality check. The one thing I realized about most corporations is that they have more than one customer. This is when multi-hustling became a critical strategy in developing my long-term objectives. I could not depend on one source of income to be financially stable. My ultimate goal was to have a day job to pay some of the bills and have my own business that I would work in my spare time. When it comes to multi-hustling, there is no spare time. In my situation my job was gone, and I had to make up for $60,000 of lost income. I applied for several jobs, but no one was hiring. At that point I decided to hire myself.

If no one will hire you, hire yourself. You will be surprised how much money you can make when you put your mind to it. I took everything I had in savings out of my account, cashed in my 401k, and went to work. The penalties for cashing out my 401k were horrific. I paid approximately 40% in taxes and penalties, which netted me approximately $3,500. With my savings, 401k, and equity in my home, I had $20,000 for survival and to start a business. One of my passions is investing in real-estate. When the real-estate market was in a "boom", I had the chance to "flip" a house. Flipping a house is buying a property for a good price, fixing it up to raise the value, and selling it for a profit. I had the chance to flip a house with my nephew and made a decent profit. While flipping this home, I learned how to install drywall. This valuable skill came in handy when I lost my job. A good friend of mine was a contractor and subcontracted several drywall installation jobs to me. Even though I was no drywall expert, my brother-in-law was. I got my brother-in-law, Earlest, and my friend, Todd, to go into business with me. If you think starting a business is expensive and complicated, think again. The only things I did were: got a business license for $40.00 from the county clerk, applied for a federal tax-ID online (which is free of charge), printed up business cards, and bought $100.00 worth of drywall material. With a $140 investment, my business was easily started. The dry walling jobs were not making me a substantial amount of money. The jobs paid on average $600.00 to $1,000, and I had to pay my business partners who did the majority of the work. Labor costs decreased my profit margin. Installing drywall was a humbling experience for me. I had gone to college to avoid manual labor. However, I am a strong believer that "pride comes before the fall."

Too often, we as individuals let our egos restrict us from acquiring wealth by any means necessary. Instead, we should humble ourselves and take a job that we normally would not. An undesired job is still income. If you have to work a fast-food job or in a grocery store to make ends meet, put your pride to the side and do what is necessary to stay legit. Work the hustle job in the day and create a grand plan at night. Remember, the day job is just another customer anyway. The next thing I decided to do was use my primary asset (my home) to make money. I decided to rent out part of my home to a relative.

The one asset I had in my home was my ability to rent out living space. Pride has kept many people from taking advantage of this opportunity. If you have available space and can't afford your rent or mortgage, move someone in to help pay the bills!

This is a business arrangement and personal relationships have to be taken out of the equation. You are the landlord, and they are your tenant. Within thirty days of being laid off, I had created two streams of income for myself. Another strategy I used as an owner was lowering my debt and expenses. If it wasn't essential for me to survive, the expense was cut out. I cut off my cable T.V., stopped my internet service, and only paid my car payment, insurance, mortgage, electric service, water service, and phone bill. These were the things I needed to function, and all of the monthly payments were extremely late.

I wasn't able to pay my credit card payments, hospital bills, and small loans. Of course, this lead to collections and a poor credit score. Even though credit is very important in the long term for financial growth, it definitely can be sacrificed in the short term to stabilize your situation. Credit can always be repaired over time, and you can always regain what you lose while trying to accomplish your goals. The things you lose should be viewed as a sacrifice for achieving long-term objectives. Once you are financially stable, you should start repairing your credit, immediately. When repairing your credit, start with the items that are in collections and pay the small items off first. Then, you should pay off larger items. The main thing is not to be overwhelmed by debt. My late grandmother use to say that a person will die owing someone, so you should not let the stress and frustration of being in debt lead you to an early grave. Understand which debts you currently have control over and make a long-term plan to control the rest. I refuse to let my mental state be controlled by money or the lack of it. In my mind, I am always rich if I can provide food and shelter for myself. If I don't have a car, there is absolutely nothing wrong with taking advantage of public transportation. Once again, you have to remove pride out of the picture when you are legal hustling. Legal hustling focuses on the long term and not the circumstances that arrive in the short term.

As I stated earlier, credit can be repaired in the long term and should be repaired as soon as possible. One of the key assets to long-term wealth is having good credit. The last thing I want to do is make anyone think credit is not important, because it is one of the tools financial institutions and employers use to determine a person's worth. To determine your credit worth, order credit reports from all three credit bureaus. This will give you an idea how good or bad your credit score is and what needs to be repaired.

To accomplish my goals, I had to make sure I had the knowledge to achieve them. To achieve your long-term goals you have to have knowledge. In my experiences I developed 10 skills that helped me get the knowledge and understanding needed to accomplish my goals. I named these skills "the 10 keys of knowledge."

The 10 keys of knowledge are:

1. Creativity
2. Networking
3. Opportunity
4. Discipline
5. Leadership
6. Education
7. God/Greatness
8. Faith
9. Focus
10. Courage

Creativity

Creativity is the "process involving the generation of new ideas or concepts, or new associations between existing ideas or concepts, and their substantiation into a product that has novelty and originality."[1] By this definition, creativity is simply having an idea. Many of which culminate from the recognition of a need. This is the basis for a good invention. In the early 20th century, the British military recognized a need for a vehicle that could take on enemy fire and maneuver through any terrain. The military tank was created to meet this need in World War I. Leonardo da Vinci was the first to design a tank, but the British capitalized on the idea and were very successful in World War I as a result. From this example, it is easy to see that creativity has won wars and can be used to win the war against poverty and hopelessness. When an individual is fighting to get a job, they are actually at war with other applicants, the organization with which they are trying to gain employment, and themselves. This requires an individual to be creative in his or her quest for employment and making potential customers (employers) recognize the need to hire the individual. When I was laid off from my job, I decided to go to war with my economic situation and created a business.

No one or nothing was going to stop me from accomplishing my goals, including myself. I had to get creative in my thought process and find a way to make money. Please, do not interpret this to mean that I went out, bought several firearms, and resorted to violence to get money. The weapon I used was my mind, which is far deadlier than any nuclear weapon.

Networking

Networking is "a supportive system of sharing information and services among individuals and groups having a common interest."[2] The common interest of multi-hustlers is making money! Networking is a key component to success in the business environment. How do you network? Talking with as many people as you can and sharing information is the easiest way to network. Music mogul Russell Simmons is well known for his networking skills. I remember watching an interview with Russell on television, and I was shocked at the ease of his networking skills and how well they worked. When Russell was trying to get Def Jam Records established in the late 1970's and early 1980's, he would go to parties and make it his priority to talk to everyone there. Regardless of whom they were or how relevant they were, he talked to them. By having this aggressive attitude, he was able to establish strong communications with his target audience and create a fan base for his artists.

Communication is the cornerstone to networking. You have to be able to put your ego to the side and talk to people you normally would not. To be an effective communicator, you have to eliminate shyness, doubt, and lack of confidence from your character. Being willing to talk to anyone who crosses your path can lead to lifetime relations that could result into making a substantial amount of money. Another example of communicating is when I got an opportunity to work with the Equal Employment Opportunity Commission (EEOC). The EEOC is a federal agency formed after the passing of the Civil Rights Act of 1964. The agency enforces the laws that were formed to eliminate discrimination in the workplace. After being laid off, I tried to use my military experience to find an opportunity in the federal system, since veterans have first preference for these positions. For nine months, I applied for at least 100 positions without a single interview. This was very discouraging to say the least. I had a very impressive resume, but no calls were coming. My good friend Laturel had recently completed a contracting job in Iraq and also applied for numerous positions. I was in Tennessee at the time, and Laturel was located in Texas. Within two months of him getting back from Iraq, he was selected for an Information Technology (IT) position in Texas. How in the world did he land a federal position in two months? I had been trying for nine months.

Laturel told me that a perfect stranger, who was also a veteran, told him the key words in the job announcements have to appear in the applicant's resume. He just happened to meet this gentleman at a hiring center for veterans, and the gentlemen was attending orientation for a job he had just secured. Laturel was frustrated about not getting a job in Texas and just happened to strike up a conversation with this gentleman. The gentlemen explained that government positions require individuals to go online and upload a resume. A computer screens the resume for key words that are in the job announcements. If a person doesn't have the key words in the resume, the computer kicks it right out.

For the longest I was battling a computer and losing, because I did not have the key words in my resume. Within a month of Laturel telling me this valuable information, I placed the key words in my resume and was hired by the EEOC a couple of months later. I benefited from someone else's good networking. A perfect stranger helped two struggling veterans get jobs. This was due to the fact that Laturel was not afraid to talk to a perfect stranger, and not too proud to pass the information to me. I haven't seen Laturel in over 10 years, but we have kept in contact and helped each other out whenever we could. This was effective networking at its best.

Opportunity

There are two definitions I would like to examine for "opportunity." The first one states an opportunity is "an appropriate or favorable time or occasion."[2] The next definition states that an opportunity is "a situation or condition favorable for attainment of a goal."[2] To put it simple, both of these definitions refer to being in the right place at the right time. The only issue I have with the first definition is the need for a "favorable time or occasion." Sometimes, an individual has to take the initiative and create the right place and right time. The second definition states the situation or condition has to be favorable. Again, individuals have to be proactive and create favorable conditions for themselves. There is no perfect condition or favorable time for accomplishing goals and making money. It makes absolutely no sense to wait on opportunity, because it will pass you by without you even knowing it.

There is an opportunity to make money every time I wake up in the morning and go into the world. When I was laid off, I did not have a clue about what I was going to do or from where my next paycheck was coming. My friend Mark was constantly on the

18

go, writing estimates for contracting jobs and managing the construction projects he had going. I decided to ask Mark if I could ride with him a few days of the week for free to get some inspiration and motivation. After a few weeks of riding with Mark, opportunity presented itself. Mark received a disturbing phone call about one of his construction projects. His primary sheetrock crew had done a terrible job hanging drywall, and the client did not want the crew back in their home.

This was my opportunity to make some money and start a business for myself. Mark fired the subcontractor, and after he calmed down from going into a tirade about his crew letting him down, I explained that my brother-in-law was a master carpenter and would be the right person to finish the drywall job. Because I had created a good rapport by riding with Mark for a few weeks, I was able to capitalize on an opportunity that I might have missed if I had not been riding with Mark for free! I could have stayed at home complaining and whining about being laid off, instead I decided to stay positive and motivated in my search for income. From this example, it is easy to recognize that the opportunity was created by me, because I decided to put myself in the right place for opportunity and not sit around and wait for an opportunity to knock on my door. To be successful, one must constantly look for opportunities as well as create situations where opportunity can find them.

Discipline

Discipline is one of my favorite keys of knowledge, because it is one of the most challenging. The definition for discipline is an "activity, exercise, or a regimen that develops or improves a skill; training."[2] The skill that must be improved when multi-hustling is discipline. An individual's thought process can be his or her biggest downfall. I think Robert De Niro said it best in the movie "Heat." De Niro's character in the movie, Neal, stated "when you call yourself making moves on the streets, have

19

nothing or no one in your life you are not willing to drop in 30 seconds flat, if you feel the heat around the corner."[3] De Niro played the role of a disciplined bank robber who always had his eye on the prize, which was the next big robbery. Of course, I am not suggesting a person drop everything, go out, and rob a bank. What I am suggesting is that De Niro's character had the right concept and drive, but the wrong hustle. An intelligent person can create positivity out of a negative situation. A positive spin can be placed on this great statement as well. In the case of multi-hustling I believe that a person should not have anyone or anything in their life they are not willing to drop in 30 seconds flat, if they sense opportunity around the corner.

In other words, you should let nothing and no one stop you from accomplishing your goals. This includes family, friends, finances, yourself, or anything else for that matter. I can't count the numerous times I thought I was in love with a beautiful woman and got completely distracted from my goals. In the end, I would lose the woman and the opportunities that came my way. This is no longer a problem for me. I have disciplined my mind to have tunnel vision, and my goals are at the end of the tunnel. If someone or something is hindering you instead of helping you, let them go! This is discipline at its best. The flesh might tell you to stay in that situation, but your disciplined mind will tell you to keep it moving.

When you're trying to accomplish your goals, you will lose friends and sometimes family. Remember, I had to streamline my expenses to get back on my feet. This was the first act of discipline that had to be done to get my finances under control. I didn't want to get rid of my cable TV, because I love watching TV! Again, things must be lost in the short term to accomplish long-term goals.

Another key to discipline is maintaining your own pace and not keeping up with someone else's. You shouldn't worry about what your neighbor has and what you don't. The same applies to your activities as well. I knew plenty of people who cut corners to accomplish the goals that I was trying to achieve, and they were participating in illegal activities to accomplish them. Legal hustling is a long-term process, and not an overnight solution. While it took me a little longer to accomplish my goals, I didn't end up in prison or dead trying to speed up the progress. When people chase fast money, they are in mental prison anyway. In the Army I use to hear the statement "stay alert, stay alive" constantly. When I began multi-hustling, this statement took on a whole new meaning. If I was disciplined and alert of my actions, I would be alive to fight and hustle another day.

Leadership

One of the best definitions for leadership is "an act or instance of leading; guidance; direction."[2] From this definition, I concluded that anyone can be a leader and possess leadership. Anyone can give directions or guidance, but the effectiveness of the directions or guidance is what sets good leaders apart from bad ones. The subject of leadership has been debated for years amongst academic scholars. Are people born with leadership? Can leadership be developed? There is no such thing as a natural-born leader. Anyone can be a leader, and everyone's leadership skills have to be developed. Some people develop quicker than others, but it is never too late to develop leadership skills. Leadership is closely correlated with persuasion. Being able to persuade or instruct others to follow directions is leadership at its core. Another important factor about leadership is that it doesn't always come from the top of the organization. This is why it's very important to recognize your leadership capabilities regardless of your position in an organization. Remember, you are the boss and your employer should be considered a customer. According to logistics expert, Jon R. Katzenbach, "the real change leaders who affect how the majority of people perform come from the ranks of middle and frontline managers."[4] Why is this? The main reason is that leadership requires a person to lead by example; and the tone and directions of one person can affect the performance of many in an organization.

When I started my subcontracting company, I had been recently unemployed and happened to stumble on an opportunity to make money. Even though I was disappointed about losing my job, I kept up a brave front to stay motivated for my team. At the time, my brother-in-law had a great job and was not dependent on the money he made with my company; but my friend Todd was unemployed like me and needed money. Everyday, Todd would come to work motivated. He would come to work laughing and joking. When we would arrive at the job, Todd would say, "let's get this money boss!" Even though Todd did not realize it, he was motivating me to perform my best and not let him down. This is the reason I could never say Todd worked for me, because he was so influential in keeping my spirits high. In a sense, he was actually leading me. I had only been out of work for one month, but Todd had been without a job for months and was still smiling everyday. On top of that, he had a wife and daughter to support! Why was I disappointed about my situation? The only person I had to take care of was me. Todd was leading by example and influenced the entire team. If I would have come to work disgusted and discouraged, that attitude would have spread like a cancer in my organization. At the same time, it took the influence of a teammate for me to get the bigger picture.

As a leader, you have to be able to inspire others to complete the task at hand; and leadership takes place at every level of an organization. Todd took ownership of his situation and influenced me to take ownership of mine. I did not become an effective leader until I stopped worrying about the things I did not have and thankful for the things I did. Because of our leadership, Todd and I were able to work the entire summer-which was the peak season for our industry. Effective leadership was absolutely the key to our success. The development of leadership skills can definitely come from life experiences.

Education

No matter how people try to avoid it, education is essential for creating wealth. Education is "the act or process of imparting or acquiring general knowledge, developing the powers of reasoning and judgment, and generally of preparing oneself intellectually for mature life."[2] The one thing I want you to notice about this definition is that school is not mentioned one time. In other words, education can be summarized as the act of gaining knowledge. One can gain knowledge in the classroom or outside of the classroom. I recognize the fact that college is not for everyone, but it should be mandatory for a person to graduate from high school or obtain a GED. My friend Chip always says, "I might not be the smartest man in the world, but I can read, write, and count." This is a very powerful statement, because so many people are missing the basic necessities required to learn.

Chip has completed some college, but he acquired his GED after he had to drop out of high school to take care of his family. However, I don't know too many people who are better with numbers than Chip. He's probably better than five of your best accountants put together, seriously. Sometimes, life puts us in situations which require tough decisions, but, regardless, one must acquire the basic tools to be successful. A substantial amount of his education was acquired on the streets of Indianapolis and in the U.S. Army later in his life. Chip did not let his circumstances dictate his life and his pursuit of knowledge. Education can be traditional or non-traditional. Of course, traditional education is receiving instructions in a formal classroom or even online in the 21st century. Non-traditional education can be just as effective when it comes to things such as on-the-job training (OJT) or picking up a book and reading it. You are practicing non-traditional education by reading this book. If a person can discipline themselves to be slow to speak and eager to listen, there is a substantial amount of knowledge that can be gained by simply listening to a person's conversation. During the slavery period of the United States, it was illegal to teach a black person how to read. Frederick Douglas learned how to read and write by watching and listening to the children of slave owners. In the Scriptures, it is written, "My people are destroyed from a lack of knowledge" (Hosea 4:6, NIV).

I believe a lack of education is self-destruction. As the definition stated, the powers of reasoning and judgment are directly linked to learning. Our brains constantly absorb knowledge and have plenty of room for it. When we stop trying to learn, we hinder our mental growth. Some of the most successful people in the world, such as the founder of Virgin Records, Richard Branson, and founder of Microsoft, Bill Gates, did not finish college. At the same time, they did not stop learning and they used life experiences for their education. To get an education, one simply has to seek and they shall find.

God/Greatness

The reason that the seventh key of knowledge consists of God and greatness is to make believers and non-believers understand the importance of believing in something greater than themselves. As far as my beliefs are concerned, I believe everything I have achieved and will achieve comes from the blessings of God. Believing in something greater than oneself gives a person hope, motivation, drive, and deliverance. Even non-believers need to find the essence of greatness as a clear model for whatever they want to achieve in their lives. The definition of God is "the one Supreme Being, the creator and ruler of the universe."[2] For me, I have reached the conclusion that if I strive for the understanding of God, His power, and glory, there is nothing I can't achieve in my life.

To stay politically correct and reach everyone, greatness needs to be explored as well. Greatness can be defined as "the state, condition, or quality of being great; as, greatness of size, greatness of mind, power, etc."[2] For example, if you are trying to become a computer-software designer and change the world, a great person to study would be Bill Gates, because he literally changed the world with the introduction of Microsoft. Gates has achieved greatness in the software industry, and someone entering this industry might want to study what gives Gates his ambition, motivation, techniques, and drive. How can a person obtain knowledge without studying the source? For me, my source of knowledge is God. For others, their source of knowledge should be someone or something greater than themselves.

Faith

According to the Scripture, "now faith is being sure of what we hope for and certain of what we do not see" (Hebrews 11:1, NIV). The secular definition of faith is "unquestioning belief that does not require proof or evidence."[5] From these two definitions of faith, it is easy to recognize the fact that you have to believe in your goals, even though you have not accomplished them or lack evidence that they will be fulfilled. If you do not have faith in yourself and your goals, how do you expect others to have faith in you and your ambitions? Faith is about confidence. There is no room for low self-esteem, doubt, or being a skeptic of your own plans. When others see your unchanging faith in yourself and your goals, they will be willing to invest and have faith in your plans as well. You have to sell yourself as an owner, and have confidence that you have the solution for the need you are trying to fill in your environment. The road to success is not going to be easy. If it was, you wouldn't know how to handle adversity when it came your way. When I started subcontracting, I did not know from where or when my next drywall job was coming, but I had unbreakable faith that it was on the way. When the 11th hour would approach with no job in sight, I would miraculously stumble upon my next job. This is because I had faith and kept looking for work. Faith requires the armor of a soldier and not the backbone of a jellyfish. To have unbreakable faith, you must recognize your levels of strength and the endurance that you did not know you possessed.

Focus

Now, I want to examine two descriptions of focus that are relevant to knowledge. The first states that focus is "a central point, as of attraction, attention, or activity."[2] The second states that focus is "the clear and sharply defined condition of an image."[2] To accomplish your goals, you must hone in on your short-term and long-term objectives like an eagle flying a mile in the air, focused on a mouse on the ground. Having a sharp focus on your goals requires a practice I refer to as "tunnel vision." I want you to imagine yourself in a five-mile tunnel with darkness all around you. The tunnel has a strong ammonia smell from the urine of thousands of bats in the tunnel. As you walk forward in the tunnel, bats are swarming around your head; urinating and defecating on your body; and the ground is sinking under your feet from all of the bat guano. Even though you have all of these distractions, you notice a dim light at the end of the tunnel which gets bigger and brighter as you walk towards it.

The purpose of this analogy is to illustrate the type of focus you must have to reach your long-term objectives. The bats are symbolic of the trials and tribulations you will encounter while trying to reach your goals. The darkness is the negativity that will surround you when trying to make your dreams come true. Every adversity you can imagine, and some you cannot, will come across your path and try to block you from accomplishing your mission. When you try to get loans from banks, many of them will deny you. When you try to sell your product or service to potential customers, many of them will slam the door in your face. When you try to tell your family and friends about your ideas and goals, many of them will laugh at you and tell you it's not going to work. When you are in the middle of your struggle and hustle, your significant other will tell you they don't want to be with you anymore. Remember, when one door closes, another door of opportunity will open. Please, do not get discouraged when adversity comes your way. Never give up! Don't let anyone or anything make you lose focus. If I had given up when I was laid off, I would have never started my subcontracting company. If I had decided to stop applying for federal positions after the 100th try, I would never have gotten my opportunity at the EEOC on the 101st try.

Trying to control your own destiny is not for the weak, so you must recognize your weaknesses and make sure your strengths are greater. Focus is closely correlated with discipline. You cannot take your mind off the main objective, which is creating wealth for yourself. Discipline requires you to have the strength to say no and let go of the things that are holding you back. Focus gives you knowledge, because you are aware of the adversities surrounding you, but smart enough to ignore them. I believe having focus is easier than maintaining discipline, because you simply have to ignore the distractions around you and see only the light at the end of the tunnel.

Courage

The last key of knowledge is the one many people struggle with the most. Courage is "the quality of mind or spirit that enables a person to face difficulty, danger, pain, etc."[2] Who likes to experience pain? I am assuming no one does, but you will endure a significant amount of pain when you decide to release yourself from the chains of despair, poverty, ignorance, and defeat. Pain is nothing more than a sign that weakness is leaving the body and mind. The more pain you learn to endure, the stronger your mind and body will become. When I was in the U.S. Army, my drill sergeants use to constantly drill in my head their definition of courage. From a military perspective, courage is the act of doing a complete 180-degree turn, facing the adversity you fear the most, and going straight at it. If you really think about it, what do you have to fear? Everyone has a date with death, so why fear death? Money can go as easy as it comes, so why fear

27

being broke? The body is made of soft flesh on the outside and breakable bones on the inside, so why fear pain? Fear rests in only one place in our bodies, in our minds. If you can master the strength and knowledge of courage in your mind, there is nothing you cannot accomplish in your life.

With no disrespect to non-believers, the only thing I fear in my life is God. My spirituality teaches me that the fear of God is the beginning of understanding Him. I have the courage to know that I can do all things with God on my side, and nothing or no one is going to stop me. If anyone or anything gets in my way, I turn into a mental freight train and run over any adversity blocking my path. My courage has given me the strength and knowledge to know failure is not an option. When I set a goal, in my mind, I refuse to lose or quit. My mind is not conditioned to accept failure, but to learn from the shortcomings and mishaps I encounter in my life. Being knowledgeable of the fact that fear, pain, and danger only exist in my mind makes my level of courage equivalent to the strength of a million men, unbreakable. To be successful in your ventures, you have to find the courage necessary to overcome adversity.

At this point, you should know who you are and how to view yourself (as a corporation); how much you are worth; how much you owe; what your credit status is; and the knowledge necessary to be successful. These tools are very powerful and should not be wasted on unnecessary conflict, negative people or situations, and meaningless efforts to make someone else wealthy. Owning yourself is taking charge of your life. This requires no money for investment, but it does require an investment of your time and the reconditioning of your mind.

NOTES:

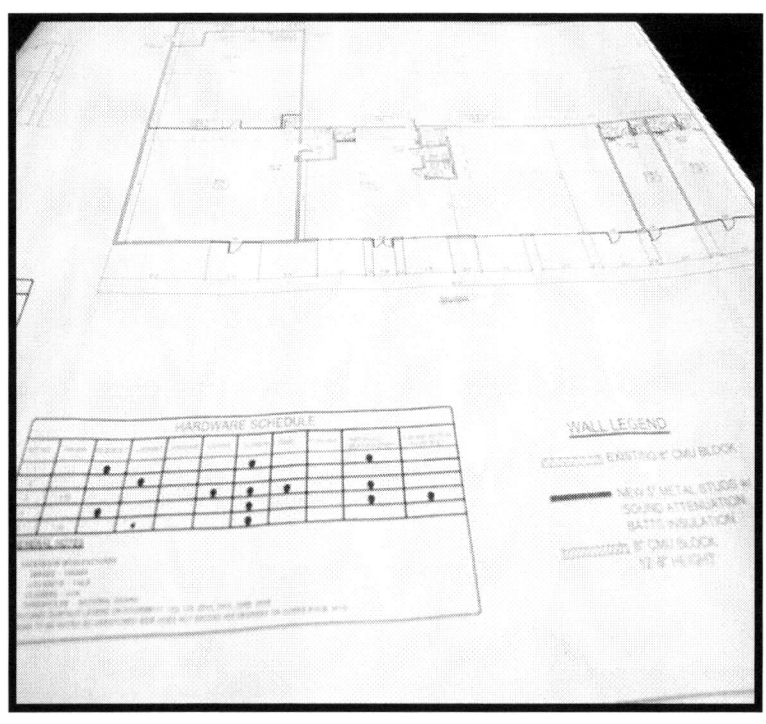

A grand plan can be viewed as a blueprint for success.

2 GRAND PLANNING

The concept of grand planning is not new to the business environment. Other names for grand planning are "master planning" or "grand strategies." Regardless of the name, the strategy is the same. Every aspect of an organization must be aligned with long-term objectives for success. I know everyone has heard the cliché "failing to plan is planning to fail." Despite this logical warning, individuals and organizations still fail to do proper planning. From my experiences, no individual or business is too small to practice definitive planning. Remember, you are now a corporation, and it's time to plan and operate like one. The strategies and concepts that are going to be discussed in this chapter have made many corporations millions of dollars. Our goal is to create a plan that will generate a six-figure income. From a business standpoint, grand planning focuses on the survival, growth, and profitability of an organization.[6] A blueprint for success has to be mapped out if an organization hopes to survive the volatile conditions of an ever-changing market. Business strategists Pearce and Robinson believe the following three factors are critical to a successful strategy:

1. The strategy must be consistent with conditions in the competitive environment
2. The strategy must place realistic requirements on the firm's resources
3. The strategy must be carefully executed[6]

These critical-success factors were designed for a corporate structure of business, but I believe any organization can benefit from these practices. These practices can also be applied to multi-hustling. When you multi-hustle, you are trying to create different sources of income at the same time. This is what Fortune 500 companies (making billions of dollars, annually) are practicing by fulfilling multiple needs for multiple target markets.

The target market is simply the base of customers you are trying to reach with your product or service.

When trying to determine the long-term objectives for a grand plan, the first item that should be addressed is the need for vision. For many organizations, "a vision statement presents the firm's strategic intent that focuses the energies and resources of the company on achieving a desirable future."[6] Regardless of the size of your organization or if you are just starting, having a vision is essential for forecasting the long-term direction in which an organization wants to go. The vision I have for my organization is for multi-hustling to become a way of life and an answer for the disenfranchised. What is your vision? Where would you like to see yourself in the next five years? There has to be an end result for whatever business ventures you decide to pursue.

Another key element to grand planning is having a mission. When organizations create a mission statement, it is often closely related to the vision statement, and the two are combined in many cases. I believe there is a clear distinction between the two. A vision statement addresses the ultimate goal for the organization. A mission statement is more focused on the needs of customers, which it should be. Remember, there is no money to be made if there are no customers. The mission for any organization should be to meet or exceed the expectations of customers. For example, a good mission statement for a restaurant would be "to provide the best-tasting food to our customers for a good price." The mission statement is often presented in places where customers can read it, such as billboards, store displays, and the Internet. The vision statement is usually found on company websites or company overviews, which are used by investors or shareholders for the purpose of examining the company as a whole. The main objective is to make sure the vision and mission are supportive of the grand plan.

When creating a grand plan, a sound environmental analysis should be conducted. An environmental analysis is often referred to as market research. A simple description of market research is gathering as much information as possible on the industry or business associated with the grand plan. Market research can make or break your long-term objectives.

For example, if you were planning to open up a barbershop in New York City, you would probably want to see how many barbershops there are in the area. In this case, you decided not to conduct market research and opened up a barbershop in New York City anyway. After being open for six months, you noticed that only 50 customers have visited your shop. If you had conducted market research, you would have known there were 10 barbershops for every square mile in New York City! Your business was a failure before it was even started, because you failed to conduct sound market research. The barbershop market in this area was clearly oversaturated.

This is just one of the mistakes people make everyday when starting a business or even applying for a job. Yes! Market research should be done on potential employers before applying for a position; this could mean the difference in you getting the job or not. Recall the situation I was in when applying for federal positions. I didn't get a position until I networked with my friend, and he gave me the vital information to be selected for the position. Networking is a form of market research, because you are gathering information.

When conducting market research, the first step that should be taken is to conduct an analysis of the internal environment. An analysis of the internal environment consists of identifying the strengths, weaknesses, opportunities, and threats of your organization. I want to continue with the example of the barbershop. This time, we're going to conduct sound market research and analyze the outcomes of both situations. Let's assume the barbershop has the following strengths:

1. Good sources of capital (cash, property, and equipment)
2. Five highly-talented barbers
3. Good location (Downtown New York City)

Capital is always important when trying to start a business. Even though banks aren't quick as they once were to offer loans, organizations such as the Small Business Association (SBA) and other organizations are willing to help entrepreneurs find funding for businesses. These organizations can easily be found in the phone book or on the Internet. Another great source of capital is finding investors. This is where networking becomes essential, and pride goes out the door. People are willing to help, but you have to be willing to ask for it. If you are able to sell yourself and your idea, finding investors is easier than you think.

The key elements of having an effective workforce are: treat employees like owners, find the best employees, pay employees well, and don't micromanage employees! With the example we are using, it's easy to make your barbers feel like owners by simply offering them ownership. This has been a tool used in the cosmetology and barber industries for years. Along with ownership, come the liabilities of risks, overhead, bills, and taxes. Some employees might not be willing to take on these responsibilities. These are the employees you don't want as partners anyway. When you decide to hire employees, try your best to find employees better than you. Internal competition and a highly-skilled workforce can lead to satisfied customers and big profits. Paying employees is self-explanatory. You also have to make sure you don't hire employees you have to micromanage. Micromanaging employees can lead to a lack of trust and low productivity.

When I think of location, the two types of businesses that come to mind are the retail and service industries. Location can be a crucial element in these industries. Your barbershop is located in New York City which has a significant amount of traffic. The best location for a retail or service business would be an area with a high volume of traffic and easily visible. After examining your strengths, you feel pretty good about your future barbershop. Now, let's assume the barbershop has the following weaknesses:

1. Lack of existing customers
2. High expenses

One of the problems you and your fellow barbers have is that all of you are fresh out of barber school. You had the idea to start a barbershop and decided to bring a few of your classmates with you. The main issue with this decision is that none of you have existing customers. This is not an uncommon situation when starting a business. A lack of customers can be overcome by a good marketing campaign to create a customer base. When you are trying to create a customer base, networking will be instrumental in your efforts to build that base.

Even though New York City is a great location, your rent for the space is $8,000 a month. With rent, taxes, utilities, and other expenses, you are now looking at operating costs totaling over $13,000 a month. To meet this obligation, you realize a customer base needs to be developed quickly. Oh yes! One of the biggest downfalls of being in an area with a high volume of traffic is the extremely high demand for that space. In most cases, locations with a high volume of traffic are hard to find. When you do find them, many people are competing to get in that location. The high cost for rent supports one of the basic laws of economics. When demand goes up and supplies are low, the price of a product or service increases. The rent is extremely high because the owners of that property know they will get the price they are asking. After identifying your strengths and weaknesses, the following opportunities need to be analyzed:

1. Offer additional services

2. Provide discounts to customers

After identifying the opportunities for your barbershop, the first thing you noticed is that there aren't very many. Even though there aren't many opportunities, they still need to be explored as part of your grand plan. In many markets, barbershops are offering other services such as manicures, pedicures, and even offering hair salon services to women. The majority of barbershop customers are men. Offering these additional services can expand the customer base, leading to higher profits. In tough economic times, everyone is looking for a discount. This could be your opportunity to corner the market with real savings and eliminate the weakness of not having existing customers. A strong marketing campaign will be the key to making potential customers aware of your additional services and customer discounts. Even though you identified only two opportunities, capitalizing on these opportunities could be the key to your success. You still need to examine the threats in your internal environment. The following threats have been identified and need to be addressed:

1. 10 barbershops exist for every square mile of New York City
2. Other barbershops in the market currently offer discounts
3. Property taxes are scheduled to increase significantly in the next six months

Now, it's getting crucial. Not only is the market oversaturated with barbershops, the failure rate for barbershops in New York City is extremely high. This is a strong enough reason, alone, to at least search for another location for the barbershop; but let's continue to explore the rest of the threats. With other barbershops also offering discounts to customers, the idea of increasing the customer base through this method might be pointless. To make matters worse, New York City has decided to raise the taxes for commercial properties. When you explored the strengths and opportunities of the internal environment, opening up a barbershop in New York City seemed like a great plan. Once you identified the weaknesses and threats in the internal environment, you realized opening up a barbershop in New York City might be more than you can handle. What you have just conducted is a SWOT analysis (strengths, weaknesses, opportunities, and threats). A SWOT analysis can identify issues early in grand planning before major decisions are made. If you had conducted a SWOT analysis in the first scenario, you would have saved a significant amount of time and money. Your decision to conduct a SWOT analysis in the second scenario helped you identify what I like to call "a grand-plan killer." I believe it's never good to start a business in an oversaturated market. If you do decide to open up a business in an oversaturated market, you have to be able to differentiate yourself from the competition and offer a product or service that is more desirable.

Now it's time to conduct market research on the external environment. This is when market research of the internal environment becomes very important. You will use the information you gathered on your organization and compare it with the trends and factors that exist in the marketplace. There are many factors that exist in the external environment, but I have identified four essential factors that you must know about the environment in which you will be operating. These factors can be referred to as "the four knows." The four knows consist of the following:

1. Know your industry
2. Know your competitors
3. Know your customers
4. Know your suppliers

Know Your Industry

When obtaining knowledge on an industry, one of the first things you want to do is identify the entry barriers of the selected industry. Entry barriers are the forces and trends that keep a new business from entering a market. One of the most common entry barriers for new businesses is high start-up costs. Let's say you decided you want to open up a McDonald's restaurant in your community. With McDonald's being a major franchise, you will have to get permission from the McDonald's corporation and pay a franchising fee to use their name, trademarks, and products. According to www.thefranchisemall.com, the total investment for opening up a McDonald's is $950,000-$1,800,000, and the initial franchise fee is $45,000.[7]

I found the website very useful for doing research on franchise businesses. This is not the only site that offered good information on franchises, and there is a significant amount of useful information you can find on the Internet when conducting market research. Opening up a McDonald's franchise is on the high end of entry-level costs. High start-up costs aren't the only entry barriers to consider. For example, if you are planning to open up any type of establishment that serves beer or liquor, you will be required to acquire a liquor and/or beer license to sell. These licenses can be expensive and not always easy to acquire. Not all entry barriers are expensive or challenging. Remember, I started my subcontracting business with $140. The main objective is identifying entry barriers early so you can develop the right strategy to tackle them.

Another key element you want to know about your operating industry is the profit margin. Profit margin is simply the percentage of net profits you have left after all taxes, expenses, and overhead have been paid. This percentage can be calculated by dividing your net profits by your total sales. A good profit margin for any industry should be around 20%. This percentage could be higher or lower, depending on the industry. Let's revisit the barbershop scenario. Examine figure 1 to see the calculation for determining net profits.

$5,000 (total sales)

-1,500 (30% tax rate)

$3,500

- 500 (weekly expenses)

$3,000

-2,000 (overhead/labor costs)

$1,000 (net profits)

Figure 1

If the barbershop made $5,000 in total sales for the week, a 20% profit margin would leave you with $1,000 in net profits ($1,000/$5,000 = 0.20 or 20%). Examining an industry's profit margin will let you know real quick if this is the industry you want to enter. If the profit margin is low, this doesn't always mean low profits. If you own a car dealership with average weekly sales of $60,000, a 5% profit margin would leave you with $3,000 in net profits for the week.

To measure the volatility of an industry, business owners have to be aware of the economic conditions that exist in the market. Economic conditions can significantly affect an industry and need to be taken into consideration. The best example of an industry being affected by economic conditions was the crisis in the housing market in 2008. Before the crisis, everyone (including myself) was trying to get in the real-estate industry. Banks and financial institutions were offering great interest rates on loans, and obtaining a loan was fairly easy. If you could find the right property and get it for a fair price, it was almost a guarantee you would make a profit when you restored the property and sold it. Besides myself, I knew at least 10 other people buying and flipping properties. The entire time I was thinking, "this is too good to be true!" Of course, the hot real-estate market was too good to be true.

The banks and financial institutions were writing bad loans, and the people they were writing these loans for did not have the income to payback the loans. Also, people were not given loans with a fixed-rate mortgage; they were giving people an adjustable-rate mortgage (ARM). The major difference in a fixed-interest rate and an adjustable rate is exactly as the names suggest. If you get a 30-year mortgage on your home and the interest rate is fixed, you do not have to worry about your payments rising due to an increase in rates that adjust periodically. If you had an ARM, your interest rate would adjust in approximately three years. People were manipulated into choosing ARMs and unaware of the problems that were heading their way.

In the 4th quarter of 2007, the ARMs began to adjust, and that is when all hell broke loose in the housing market. For example, if you were paying $800 a month for the past three years on your mortgage, you were more than likely to see your mortgage increase to $1,600 a month or more in many cases. People who get ARMs are usually investors and plan to sell the property within one to three years. You have to educate yourself on any major investment decision and read the fine print in all contracts. Never be in a rush to sign anything. When you rush to make a decision, it's usually the wrong decision. When you conduct the proper research, you should know how strong or weak an industry is, and it is never a good idea to enter an industry that has a significant amount of problems or is in a serious decline.

Know Your Competitors

Knowing your competitors is crucial when analyzing the external environment. One of the best ways to identify competitors is through a process called benchmarking. According to a leading logistics expert, Rob Martinez, this process is essential to any organization; he also states that "benchmarking is a core component of business improvement…monitor your company's internal measurements and compare the data with other leading organizations."[8] In other words, benchmarking is researching and analyzing every aspect of your competitors and knowing how your organization compares. Martinez believes benchmarking should be done in five critical steps:

1. Planning
2. Data collection
3. Analysis
4. Recommendation/implementation
5. Monitoring[8]

These steps are somewhat self-explanatory, but they still need to be explained in detail. "Planning" consists of identifying your competitors and figuring out what research you're going to do on the competition. Martinez suggested that, to benchmark, an organization identifies the leading competitors. I agree with this concept, but I think an organization will get a better analysis of its competitors by analyzing the best, average, and worst competitors in a given market. Why? When you benchmark the best competitor, it gives a clear example of how your organization needs to perform to be a market leader and quickly identifies what improvements your organization needs to make. When the average competitor is benchmarked, it gives you the standard performance of competitors in a given market and where your organization should be, competitively. When you benchmark the worst competitor in a given market, it gives you a clear indication of where you don't want to be in the market, and it should also identify mistakes the competitor is making. You should make sure to avoid these mistakes at all costs.

Once you have identified which competitors you are going to benchmark, start figuring out what information you are going to analyze. The type of data you want to collect on your competitors depends on your industry and the crucial factors of that industry. From my experience, you should at least analyze the competitors' pricing, annual sales, customer satisfaction ratings, profit margins, years in business, operating costs, and organizational setups. A substantial amount of this information is a matter of public record and should be easy to obtain.

The next step in benchmarking is data collection. As mentioned earlier, a competitor's information can be easily obtained if you are looking in the right place. Martinez identified the following sources for gathering data on competitors: industry associations, networking groups, research studies, consultants, universities, industry periodicals, government data, libraries and online databases.[8] With this long list of sources, there is no excuse for not being able to gather information on your competitors, especially with the Internet readily available! I don't want to hear the excuse of not having Internet access at home. Go to the library! The library is sitting there waiting for you to enter and gather as much information as you can. Many libraries have free internet access and only require a library membership to use their services.

Once you have gathered all the data you want to collect on your competitors, it's time to analyze it. The best way to analyze the data is gather the same information on your organization and compare it with your competitors' information. Identify what you are doing better than your competitors and what you are doing worse than your competitors. Another key component to your analysis is what your competitors are doing which you are not. If the competition is outperforming your organization, these differences could be the reason why. If you are charging $25 for a haircut and your competitor is charging $15 for a haircut with a free shave, this might be a clear indication why the competitor has more customers than your organization. Key observations such as this one can help you stay competitive in the long run.

Now it is time to make recommendations and implement based on the analyzed data. You have identified the differences between your organization and the competition. This would be a good time to make some changes if your competitors are performing better than you. The first thing you should do is identify what is going right with your competitors and capitalize on this information. You should create opportunities to improve on your competitions' strategies or implement a new and improved strategy all together. Remember, you want to avoid everything that has had a negative impact on the competition and make plans not to repeat their mistakes.

Once you have identified and made the necessary changes after benchmarking, constantly monitor these changes to see what type of impact they have on your organization and the competition. This will let you know if the improvements are helping or hindering your organization. There is no way to get a good analysis of a given market without benchmarking the competition. How can you go to war when you know nothing about your enemy? It doesn't make sense from a military standpoint, and it definitely doesn't make sense from a business standpoint. Benchmarking is not a short process but a lengthy one. It should be a long and calculated process. This is the only way you are going to get quality data on your competitors. The use of benchmarking can save you a significant amount of time and money in the long term by avoiding the mistakes others have made. After performing your first benchmark, the process will get easier, and the time it takes to benchmark should decrease.

Know Your Customers

When conducting market research in the external environment, the third component of this process is to know your customers. The first thing you want to identify about your customers is: who they are. Do this by identifying your target market. As mentioned earlier, the target market is simply the base of customers you are trying to reach with your product or service. To identify your target market, you need to examine the demographics of your customers. Demographics describe the characteristics of the target market such as age, gender, ethnicity, income, and occupation.[9] To get a better understanding of demographics, the following table describes the characteristics that should be identified in a demographic analysis:

Demographic	Characteristics
Gender	Male; female
Age	Under 6 yrs; 6-11 yrs; 12-17 yrs; 18-24 yrs; 25-34 yrs; 35-44 yrs; 45-54 yrs; 55-64 yrs; 65-74 yrs; 75 yrs plus
Race	African-American; Asian; Hispanic; White/Caucasian; etc
Life stage	Infant; preschool; child; youth; collegiate; adult; senior
Birth era	Baby boomer (1949-1964); Generation X (1965-1976); Generation Y (1977-present)
Household size	1; 2; 3-4; 5 or more
Residential status	Own home; rent home

Marital status	Never married; married; separated; divorced; widowed

Table 1[9]

A sound demographic analysis can help you identify the segments or groups in the target market which you want to reach. It can also eliminate the segments or groups in the target market that are irrelevant and least likely to desire your products and services. For example, if you are trying to identify the segments or groups you would like to reach to sell home insurance, you probably want to eliminate renters from your target market. On the other hand, you probably would want to eliminate home owners from your target market if you are selling renter's insurance. Obtaining demographic information on your target market can be achieved in different ways. One of the primary strategies for obtaining demographic information is the use of surveys. A survey can be conducted by creating a questionnaire asking demographic questions. In your questionnaire, you would ask simple questions such as what is your gender; what is your age; and what is your race? After each question, provide answers with the demographic choices desired. Many organizations choose to hire professional marketing firms to create and conduct surveys. You can create and conduct surveys yourself as long as you know what questions you want to ask your target market.

To reach the target market with your surveys, you can identify the zip codes your target market resides and obtain a list with addresses of the people who reside in your target market. This information can be found on the Internet. The website that I found very useful for gathering information was www.whitepages.com.[10] After you have obtained your list, simply mail your surveys to people in the identified target market. Of course, people are hesitant to release demographic information with the threat of identity theft in the 21st century. Try to refrain from asking for names and other indentifying information. If you are trying to control costs and have a small organization, you could always get in your car and drive through the target market. I will often get in my truck and drive through my city and identify homes for sale, construction projects, rental properties, and the types of people who make up my city. This method will definitely cut down on cost and time compared to the process it takes to conduct a survey. If you don't have a car, borrow one or ride the bus. There is no room for excuses.

Another critical factor that you want to identify in your target market is "need." You want to identify a need in your target market that is currently not being fulfilled. For example, if you want to open up a Chinese restaurant, you want to identify an area where there are no Chinese restaurants. If 60% of your target market are Asian Americans who drive across town to get to the closest Asian restaurant, you have just identified a need for a Chinese restaurant in the immediate area. Before you choose to open up a Chinese restaurant, you might want to check and make sure that no other Asian nationalities make up the majority of that 60%. The reason I gave this example is to show that the more research you do, the less likely you are to fail at identifying your target market. You can discover a need in your external environment by simply looking around your area and identify what is missing. Once you have identified that need, you need to be the first one to fulfill it. Being observant of your surroundings can lead to good ideas and strategies for accomplishing your long-term objectives. Knowing your customers is essential to meeting or exceeding their expectations. If you do not know every relevant aspect of your target market, there is no way you can fulfill the needs of your customers.

Know Your Suppliers

The last factor is to know your suppliers. Who are your suppliers? Your suppliers are anyone who provides your organization with products, equipment, or services that you can not provide yourself. For example, if you can not provide your own water to run your business, then the local water company is a supplier. If you can not provide your own electricity to run your business, then the local electric company is a supplier. If you can not make the paper plates you use in your restaurant, then the place where you buy your paper plates is a supplier. Another key factor about your supply chain that you want to know is the number of available suppliers you have. In some instances, such as utility suppliers, you will only have one. Unfortunately, there is only one electric or water company in many areas. In some cities, utilities such as electric and natural gas are combined. When you do have several choices for suppliers, you always want to get the best price and quality to keep costs low. There is nothing wrong with getting suppliers to compete for your business. As long as you get the best price, a bidding war amongst suppliers only benefits you.

You also want to make sure your supplier is reliable and not just the lowest bidder. If you are running a restaurant and your meat supplier is constantly late or short on your orders, the supplier could ultimately ruin your business. A good way to check the reliability of your suppliers is to get feedback from their customers. The number of customers a supplier has could be a good indication of their reliability as well. Once you have found reliable suppliers, develop a good rapport with them. This will ensure reliability and create loyalty as well. The four knows can be applied to an existing business or a business in the planning stages. Regardless, this information is essential to properly examine your target market and capitalize on the research gathered. Research is where the money is. Information is valuable and worth the time taken to gather it.

"Focusing on long-term objectives is the key to success."

3 SHORT AND LONG-TERM OBJECTIVES

The one common factor I noticed in my pursuit for a $100,000 income and the individuals I studied making $100,000 is the focus on long-term objectives. Focusing on long-term objectives is the key to success. Long-term planning needs to be addressed before short-term planning can even be considered. This might seem like a backwards approach, but there is a strategic explanation for this type of planning. When you are grand planning, short-term objectives are created to strategically support long-term objectives. In other words long-term objectives are the end results of grand planning, and short-term objectives make up the blueprint on how to reach end results. Another key difference between short-term and long-term objectives is the timeline. Grand plans that are created in the short-term are for a period of less than one year, and the timeline for long-term objectives is usually from a period of two to five years.

The ultimate goal of long-term planning is to create a competitive advantage in the target market. Creating a competitive advantage is one of my favorite topics in business management. When an organization is able to create a competitive advantage, it corners a market and becomes the only one that can offer a particular product or service under certain conditions. Under these conditions a competitive advantage exists when an organization is able to meet or exceed the expectations of its customers, and competitors can not duplicate or imitate the same success in the long-run.[11] This means you have created a product or service that can not be copied by your competitors for at least two to five years, maybe even longer in some cases. For this period, you have gained a competitive advantage. Not only would you have a sustained competitive advantage, but you would be able to make higher profits and dominate the competition. Michael Porter, one of the leading experts on the concept of this subject, believes a competitive advantage is created by adopting one of the following three strategies:

1. Focusing on becoming the overall low-cost leader in an industry
2. Focusing on the creation and marketing of unique products for varied customer groups through differentiation
3. Focusing on having special appeal to one or more groups of consumer or industrial buyers, concentrating on their cost or differentiation concerns[6]

Being a low-cost leader in an industry means an organization offers a product or service for a lower price. The organization is also able to produce the product or service cheaper than the competition. This is definitely a win-win situation. Competitors cannot beat the price you set for your product or service, and it costs the competition more to produce the same product or service. When I examine the illegal activities that exist in our communities, I realize that this is a practice that has been in effect for a long time. Drug dealers practice this same concept. They purchase and sell illegal drugs for the cheapest price, lower than the competition. There are geniuses on the streets in our communities. For many drug dealers, if they had taken another path and applied their ambitions and creativity to a legal hustle, many of them would be Chief Executive Officers (CEOs) of Fortune 500 companies and making millions of dollars, (maybe even billions) legally! These men and women have mastered the concept of supply and demand without taking a single economics course, but they are offering the wrong product and service to our communities.

What if these geniuses would realize their mistakes and decided to legal hustle instead of selling drugs? If this was to take place, I believe our communities would be a much safer place and more prosperous in the long run. For my brothers and sisters still participating in illegal activities, there is nothing wrong with your aim. It's just time to change your target. Life deals everyone some rough cards sometimes, and people find themselves in situations in which they really don't want to be. Target a bigger market that has bigger profits. Not only is the legal market bigger with substantially larger profits, but it keeps you alive and out of prison. The time for change has come, and the change has to come from within.

The second factor for creating a competitive advantage is differentiating your product or service from the competition. An excellent example of this practice would be the automobile wars of the 1980s. In the 1980s Japanese car manufacturers hit the U.S. market hard with their products. The Japanese were beginning to gain large segments of the U.S. market from American car manufactures. How did this happen? This was a result of a practice called Total Quality Management (TQM). TQM is a management philosophy that focuses on implementing the highest level of quality at every stage of creating a product or service. From the beginning to the end of the creation of a product or service, quality has to be the highest priority. This is what the Japanese practiced in the manufacturing of their cars. When the Japanese began to manufacture cars everything was important, from the screw that holds the headlight in place to the type of metal used on the bumper.

With this practice, Japanese car makers began to build cars that would last over 20 years compared to the five or six years an American car would last. Throughout the late 1970s into the mid 1980s, American cars were built to last until a customer had ultimately paid a car off. I used to hear my dad complaining about him not having any problems out of his cars until he was one year out from paying it off. When the American car was finally paid off, it was time to go and buy another one because the car was in terrible condition. Japanese automakers had been selling cars in the U.S. since the 1970s, but it wasn't until the 1980s that consumers realized that their cars, after being paid off, were still running. In many cases, the cars were running as good as the first day they were purchased. Americans started to take notice of the reliability and longevity of Japanese cars, and the demand for these cars exploded. What was the difference between American and Japanese cars? Quality was the difference, and the Japanese created a competitive advantage in the U.S. car industry with this quality. The American car manufacturers did not catch on to this concept until the late 1980s. By this time, it was almost too late. I believe Ford was the first car manufacturer to catch on to this concept. In the late 1980s and early 1990s, Ford adopted a new motto of "Quality is job #1". If you noticed, the Japanese held a competitive advantage for approximately 10 years before American car manufactures recognized the need to increase the quality and reliability of their cars. What is different about your product or service, and can it dominate the target market? These are the questions you need to ask when trying to create a competitive advantage through differentiation.

The last factor for creating a competitive advantage is having an appealing product or service in the target market, by addressing the cost and differentiation concerns of customers. I recently saw a commercial on TV that clearly addresses this focus. If you have ever had to purchase ink for a small printer, you know the cost of replacing ink cartridges is outrageous. An ink cartridge costs an average of $30. Many customers have been complaining about the high cost of replacing ink cartridges and are always searching for lower prices. In the commercial a company is introducing a new printer to the market that will offer ink cartridges for less than $5. Not only have they cut the cost of ink by more than 80%, but they have introduced a new product along with the cheaper ink cartridges. Competitors cannot duplicate this idea for awhile, because their printers use the expensive ink cartridges, exclusively.

The primary way to gain a competitive advantage is recognizing a need that already exists in the market and fulfilling that need, with special appeal. Unlike the first two factors of a competitive advantage, the need was already in the market without having to make customers recognize a need for change. In the second example, the need for more quality cars existed, but customers did not recognize the need for change. In the case of the ink cartridges, customers recognized the need and were demanding change on their own. The low cost to replace the ink cartridges is very appealing to customers. In order for competitors to duplicate this product, they will have to design a new printer, offer a cheaper ink cartridge, then introduce both products to the market for a competitive price. This could take at least a couple of years to accomplish! Fulfilling an existing need in the target market is more effective than identifying a need in the target market and making customers aware of that need.

Once you have identified an opportunity to create a competitive advantage in your target market, then you have to set long-term objectives to sustain the competitive advantage. According to Porter, long-term objectives need to have the following seven qualities:

1. The objectives need to be accepted by the leadership of the organization.
2. The objectives have to be flexible and adaptable to changes that will occur in the internal and external environment
3. The objectives have to be measurable by clearly stating what will be achieved and when it will be achieved
4. The objectives must be motivating to the entire organization
5. The objectives have to be aligned with the mission statement of the organization
6. The objectives have to be understood by the leadership in the organization
7. The objectives have to be realistic and achievable by the organization[6]

When long-term objectives are developed, the leadership of the organization will be the ones to make sure they are accomplished. This is why anyone in a leadership position in your organization has to be willing to accept this responsibility. The leaders must believe in the objectives and take ownership of them. Too often, leaders are asked to achieve objectives that are completely irrelevant to their function in the organization. Leaders must believe their success is closely correlated with long-term objectives.

As discussed earlier, the internal and external environments of an organization are constantly changing. Long-term objectives must be adaptable and ready for this constant change. A good example of this would be operating costs. When most companies enter an industry, the initial operating costs to produce a product or service might be lower than the operating costs to produce the same product or service in the future. Companies have to plan for fluctuations in operating costs and avoid losing profits when operating costs adjust in the future. If you decided to open up a moving company, you need to anticipate the price of fuel rising in the future. If a gallon of fuel rises by 25% every two years, you need to plan for this increase. Have you ever noticed a fuel cost on your electric bill? It's more likely that this fuel cost has been averaged over the next two years, and the electric company has passed the anticipated cost increase of fuel off to you. When the cost of fuel does actually increase, the electric company has already prepared for it by having you pay for it.

A timeline must be set for long-term objectives. When I decided to set a long-term objective of making $100,000 in sales, I gave myself two years to accomplish this goal. The goal was set, and the clock was ticking. Everyone in my organization was aware of the timeline and understood what was at stake to accomplish this goal. Not only is it important to set realistic timelines for achieving long-term objectives, the entire organization needs to be aware of the timeline.

Long-term objectives have to be motivating and inspire the entire organization. When an organization is motivated, it has higher productivity. If the members of an organization are motivated about the products and services they are delivering, then the expectations of the customers receiving the products or services will be met or exceeded. If the mission statement does not support the long-term objectives of the organization, then it is meaningless. Remember, the ultimate goal of long-term objectives is fulfill the needs of the target market. Since the mission statement is customer focused, long-term objectives must be aligned with the mission of the organization.

The first step in creating long-term objectives is to identify the leaders of an organization who will accomplish the goals. If the leaders don't understand the long-term objectives, how can they accomplish them? You would think this would be self explanatory, but leaders often try to accomplish objectives they do not understand. As the executive leader of your organization, you have to constantly get feedback from your leaders to make sure the mission is understood. This is one of the reasons I do not like a "yes" person in my organization. If I have someone on my team who constantly tells me what I want to hear, then I will never get the truth about how my organization is progressing. Feedback from your leaders will be the true indicator of whether long-term objectives are getting accomplished.

Long-term objectives have to be realistic and within reach. If you own one ice cream truck with one worker, would it be smart to believe you and your worker are going to make $10 million in three years? Not only do long-term objectives have to be realistic and achievable, but they can't be too easy to accomplish either. Setting mediocre goals can hinder an organization from developing strength, knowledge, and longevity in the target market. When you are able to add quality to your long-term objectives, the projected picture of your grand plan should be more in focus. Adopting these seven qualities in your long-term planning will definitely get you to see the bigger picture, and your organization will be battle-focused on the tasks at hand. At this point, your dreams are on their way to becoming reality. After an organization has developed its long-term objectives, it is time to develop an immediate plan to accomplish these goals. This is when short-term objectives are developed.

As mentioned earlier, short-term objectives have a timeline of less than one year and have to be strategically aligned with long-term objectives. Long-term plans are put into action with short-term objectives. There are four primary factors that must be addressed in the short term which I refer to as the four M's:

1. Marketing
2. Milestones
3. Mobilization
4. Motivation

Marketing

Marketing is very important in the short term and can be defined as the process of planning and the execution of pricing, promotion, and distribution of a product or service to the target market.[8] This is when market research becomes extremely valuable to the grand plan. If you conducted sound market research, you should know the average price for your product or service; who your target market is; where your potential customers are located; and the best way to distribute your product or service to the target market. Short-term planning is when you create your marketing campaign. Marketing can be very expensive and account for substantial amount of your operating budget. When starting a business, a marketing campaign should be as aggressive, effective, and efficient as possible. When I decided to market my business, I decided to practice a type of marketing that is known as "gorilla marketing."

Gorilla marketing is exactly what the name suggests; it's very flexible, aggressive, and powerful. When you plan it right, gorilla marketing is fairly cheap as well. You have to get the word out about your product or service by any means necessary. When I decided to start my business, I created flyers as part of my gorilla marketing. I didn't spend a fortune on these flyers. The flyers had my basic services typed on a sheet, and I made several copies of the flyers at Kinko's. The first thing I did to advertise my business was to distribute my flyers everywhere I knew my target market would be. I went to the home improvement stores, placed them on the doors of houses and cars, and I mailed flyers to potential customers as well. Warning: it is a federal offense to open mailboxes and place flyers. The only people authorized to open a mailbox is an employee of the U.S. Postal Service or the occupant(s) of that address. Even though it took a few weeks before I received hits from my flyers, they did come. Word-of-mouth is a form of gorilla marketing and a very powerful marketing tool as well. If you are able to deliver quality in your products and services, the word will get around. With any type of marketing campaign, you have to be patient and able to measure its effectiveness.

Milestones

A good way to measure the progress of your short-term objectives is to set milestones. Milestones are key events in grand planning that indicate progress is being made and the plan is on track. For example, I had to set milestones to let me know the progress of my $100,000 plan. I divided each year into four parts which are referred to as quarters. Giving myself two years to accomplish this objective, I had a total of eight quarters to accomplish my long-term objective. Every three months, I needed to reach a milestone of $12,500 in profits. Anytime I missed a milestone, it was time to assess the problem and see why I fell short of my goal.

Milestones are essential in short-term planning, and you can see how my milestone was strategically aligned with my long-term objective. Another example of a milestone is tracking the progress of a house being built. The long-term objective in this case is to have a house completely built in two years. By the end of the first month, the foundation for the house has been laid. This is a milestone. Another key milestone could be the installation of the electrical system. Milestones are crucial for keeping a grand plan on schedule, within budget, and focused on primary objectives.

Mobilization

The third factor of short-term objectives is the mobilization of the grand plan. Mobilization is the launching pad for the grand plan and focuses on the execution of daily tasks. When I was subcontracting, bidding on a drywall job and winning the bid was just the first part of the task. Once the bid was won, I had to coordinate every activity to initiate the job. The arrival of supplies had to be coordinated to arrive on the job site at a certain time. The mud used to install drywall had to have time to dry, and I had to plan activities around the drying period. If I did not properly plan my activities around my drying time, I would end up with idle time.

Idle time is one of the worst events that can occur in a grand plan. When you have idle time, employees are sitting around doing nothing and getting paid for it, and this is not good. While my mud was drying, I would use this time to clean up, take measurements, cut drywall, or have a meeting on what still needed to be accomplished. Productivity should never stop because another task is being completed. Continuous productivity is essential to effective multi-hustling. I didn't even allow myself to have idle time. If a saw a project meeting all of its milestones and the job was coming close to completion, then it was time for me to leave the job site and hunt for the next job. This is why I would stumble upon my next job, because I kept my operations moving and never stopped working. If you are not out working and capitalizing on every opportunity, someone else will.

Motivation

The final factor of short-term objectives is motivation. Motivation takes on a different meaning than it did in long-term planning. In the long-term, motivation is more or less a philosophical approach taken by inspiring others to accomplish a shared dream. Motivation in the short-term involves creating an awards system and compensating the supporting cast for its efforts. In other words, its time to put your money where your mouth is! Money is a major motivator in the short-term, but I prefer to empower as well as compensate the members of my team. One effective way I found that significantly motivated my team was offering ownership.

In the beginning, I didn't have a lot of money to pay my employees. In subcontracting, the profit margin is low. Approximately 10% of your revenue goes to profits, and an additional 10% of the revenue goes to overhead. Overhead is basically what you pay employees. I actually received a 5% profit, because I gave the other 5% of the profits to my employees. With this 5%, employees were now owners in my company. Owners definitely have higher productivity than employees, because their bottom line is closely correlated with the success of the company. Now, you can't offer ownership to every employee, because everyone doesn't want to be an owner. For the ones that do take on the responsibility of ownership, the accomplishment of long-term goals becomes a high priority.

Now, I have given you a substantial amount of information for creating a grand plan. The grand plan needs to be detailed and realistic to the end users of the plan which are the leaders of your organization. If you now have a good understanding of grand planning, you probably just saved yourself about $30,000 in tuition. That is how much I paid to get the same information when I got my master's degree in business administration. Grand planning is the type of strategic planning that turned Microsoft into a multi-billion dollar corporation. If Fortune 500 companies can make billions of dollars with this type of detailed planning, why can't you create a competitive advantage in your target market and make $100,000?

PART II

THE BUILDING

4 FROM PRISON TO PROSPERITY: THE CONTRACTOR

I decided to begin my case studies with a gentleman who I greatly admire and has showed me how to make serious money. When I first met Mark, I almost made the crucial mistake of judging a book by its cover. I was having a bad day because the roof on my house was leaking from a recent thunderstorm that passed through my area. At the time, I was a dispatcher for a trucking company and working the graveyard shift. I refer to the time I spent in the trucking industry as the vampire years, due to the fact that I worked at night and slept during the day. On this particular day I could not sleep. I was worried about my roof, worried about getting the money to fix it, and worried about a bunch of other meaningless things.

Since I could not sleep, it was blazing hot outside, and my air conditioner was barely putting out cool air, I decided to go down the street to the gas station and buy an ice-cold beer. When I was in line to purchase my beer, there was this weird guy in front of me. From what I could tell, he wasn't buying anything. His cloths were dirty and he was talking a lot. In my mind, I just knew this guy was intoxicated because his face was beak red and he wouldn't shut up! Now that I think about it, I had some nerve passing judgment on this man while I had a beer in my hand. While I was waiting, this man just kept talking. I was thinking to myself, "Why doesn't this guy just shut up and get out of the store?" Finally, the man started to leave and told the clerk, "Man, I got to get a move on, because I got five roof estimates to give!"

Around this time I noticed he had gotten into a nice Ford F-250, so he couldn't be that big of a drunk. Something in my mind told me to go and talk to the gentleman. I left my beer sitting on the counter and walked up to his truck. I asked him if he did roof work, and he said in a peculiar, high voice, "Man! Do I do roof jobs? I'm the best in the city!" He went on to explain that he was a general contractor and owned a construction company. He continued to explain that roofing was his specialty, and that he would come and check out my roof. After talking with him in the parking lot for awhile, I realized he wasn't drunk but dirty and sunburned from climbing on roofs all day in the hot sun. Mark also told me to get two more estimates before I made a major decision. Not only were the other roofing companies extremely expensive, but they were not willing to work with me on my insurance deductible. Even though I had insurance on my home, I did not have the money to pay my deductible at the time. Not only did Mark have the lowest bid, but he allowed me to pay my deductible in installments. I truly believe that it was God telling me to go and talk to Mark that day at the store.

Mark Musgrove, CEO of Musgrove Construction

While I was standing there judging Mark that day in the store, I had no idea that the man in front of me was a millionaire. I thought I was better than him, and he made more money in a week than I made in a year. What if I had blown the man off because I thought he was a drunk and never said anything to him? I would have missed an opportunity to meet someone who could show me how to get serious money in the future. Never judge a book by its cover. You have to be willing to network anytime, anyplace, and with anyone; you never know who God will send across your path. Mark and I have known each other for a few years now, and he actually was the reason I was able to survive my layoff. As I mentioned earlier, he was the one who gave me my break and got me into the subcontracting business. The more I learned from Mark, the more I wanted to know. Other than the big drug dealers I knew growing up, Mark was the first millionaire I had known who had become one, legally.

Even though Mark was a millionaire now, he wasn't always one. He actually had humble beginnings and was addicted to drugs at one time. His addiction eventually landed him in prison, but he was able to overcome many obstacles and became very successful. When I first began the process of selecting individuals for my case studies, I didn't want to study anyone who had not struggled and seen hard times. Everyone I wanted to study had to have a struggle, an awakening, and a legal hustle that culminated into success. Mark met every one of these criteria. I had to get his story because it was so inspiring to me, and I knew it could be inspiring and life-changing to others. When it comes to struggling, Mark is not stranger to hard times and difficult situations. At the early age of 14, his father told him it was time for him to get a job and help out the family. Mark's father dropped out of school at 16 to join the U.S. Army and help out his family. This is how his father developed a strong work ethic, and he wanted to instill the same work ethic into his children. Even though Mark started working at the age of 14, school was still a first priority. After graduating high school, he was hired by a large bread company to work in the factory. Mark was 18 and very ambitious about learning every job in the factory. Not only did he learn every job in the factory, but his boss wanted him to begin training to be in management. The last thing that was going through Mark's mind was management. At the time, he was fresh out of high school and was into chasing women and rebuilding cars. In the beginning, he was very smart about how he spent and invested his money. When he was 21, he bought a two-story house and converted it into a triplex.

By this time, Mark had a good job, a nice Corvette he rebuilt, and his own house. He rented two apartments in the triplex and lived in the third one. This allowed him to live there for free. The entire time Mark was working at the bread company, he wanted to get out and work for himself. The only problem was that he didn't know what business to get into that could equal the pay of his job. Since he had completely restored and converted his house into a triplex, the remodeling business seemed like a good industry to enter. One day, while on his lunch break, he ran into his good friend Ray, who owned a few convenient stores and remodeled houses. Mark was at one of Ray's stores when he noticed a brand new Corvette outside. He knew it probably belonged to Ray because the man kept a new car and a pocket full of cash. Ray was a millionaire and knew the hustle of making money. Even though Mark owned a Corvette, it was rebuilt and a few years old.

Mark proceeded to go into the store and saw Ray in there. He asked Ray how was he able to drive brand new Corvettes and make good money all the time. Ray told him, "Mark, you'll never be a millionaire working for someone else and stuck working a job all day." He continued to tell Mark he made his money by meeting and talking with people who introduced him to remodeling houses. Since Ray was familiar with Mark's work on his triplex and a few more jobs he had done, he told him to look into becoming a general contractor. The reason he told Mark this was that he knew how talented

Mark was and didn't want to see him waste that talent working for someone else. Mark knew Ray was right, but it just didn't sink into his head to go ahead and do it.

For a while Mark was living the American dream, until he developed a few bad habits by the time he was 23. He started using and selling crack cocaine, and that is when his troubles began. By the time he was 28, the drugs had started to take over Mark's life. After 10 years, he quit his job to do construction and sell drugs. Even though he had quit his job, he was independent and could sell anything to anybody. Mark claims that this is when he discovered the skill of being able to talk to anyone and sell any product or service.

While his drug business was taking off, his drug habit was taking off as well. He was making poor and dangerous decisions that would eventually set him up for a great fall. The day Mark got arrested for selling drugs started off normal, like any other day. He woke up next to a woman he barely remembered and had been smoking crack with her all night. After he had kicked her out, he made a couple of crack sales that morning. If you know anything about the illegal drug trade, selling drugs is a 24/7 operation. After making a little money from the transactions, he headed out to finish up a roof job. What he did not know was that his partner had sold six pounds of marijuana to an undercover narcotics agent while he was at work. Mark got home that night at approximately 6pm. When he got home, he started preparing to throw a dope party. A dope party is when he would invite a few drug addicts over to sell them drugs and get high with them. Mark said he had a very uneasy feeling the entire day and did not know why. When he was home, he started to get over his uneasiness and was ready for his party. He still noticed that something was not right about the night. Normally, Mark would have addicts waiting outside his door when he got home. Everybody came to his dope parties, but no one showed up this particular night. He still did not pay it any mind.

To prepare for his party, Mark went into his briefcase and brought out a triple-beam scale along with two ounces of cocaine, about 50 prescription painkillers, and an ounce of marijuana. He put the scale and the drugs on the top of his fireplace, sat back in his chair, and waited for the people to show up. While waiting, he decided to take a few hits off of a joint and fired up the crack pipe. Mark was determined there was going to be a party regardless. Around 8pm, someone finally knocked on the door, and he jumped up to answer it. The only thing that was going through his mind was getting high and making money. He didn't even bother to look to see who it was. Everybody in the neighborhood knew Mark and his reputation. He was a fiery redhead who was known for keeping a .45 caliber pistol on his side and a sawed-off shotgun by the front door.

As soon as Mark opened the door, a narcotics agent stuck a shotgun in his face and slammed him to the ground. The agent also had about 10 of his police buddies with him, and they had guns drawn as well. The first things the agents saw were a triple-beam scale, cocaine, pills, and marijuana on the fireplace. Mark was done. He had quit his job, and drugs completely had his mind at this point. After thousands of dollars paid to his lawyer, he received a three-year sentence in prison for three felony drug charges. He was facing nine charges and 10 years in prison, so he considered himself very blessed for not getting more time. Mark actually thought he was going to end up dead before he saw a prison cell. I guess he was wrong.

According to Mark, going to prison saved his life. While he was in prison, Mark had a moment of enlightenment and found the Lord. He hasn't looked back since and credits his success to turning his life over to Jesus. After Mark's enlightenment, the only thing he could think about was getting out of prison and changing his life. Even though he had lost his freedom, Mark believes that prison broke him from his addiction to drugs. His mind was free, and he could finally think clearly. I have often heard that there are a significant number of talented and intelligent individuals in prison. Mark confirmed that for me and was no exception. Many of the inmates Mark was incarcerated with were highly intelligent and had the skills for legitimate jobs. Why were so many of these talented people behind bars? A drug-related conviction was the reason many of them were serving time, including Mark.

Even though the most common conviction for a drug offense is possession and not the intent to resale, drugs take over the minds of good people, and they end up making a wrong decision to get their hands on drugs. Too often, a drug addiction will cause a person who has never committed a crime in his or her life to rob, steal, or even kill to get high. Just because someone goes to prison doesn't mean they lack intelligence or that they are a bad person. At the same time, too many people are making bad decisions to get high or get someone else high which end up costing them their freedom or life. When Mark was incarcerated, he got along with everyone and received some good advice from one of his fellow inmates. One day, Mark and a group of inmates were discussing what skills and talents they possessed besides the ones associated with their criminal careers. The subject of construction came up, and the other inmates were shocked by how much Mark knew about construction. One of the inmates, who was serving a life sentence for murder, got upset with Mark. He got upset with Mark for letting his skills go to waste by ending up in prison.

The inmate told Mark that he should get a general contractor's license when he got out, and he would never see prison again if he got one. This was the second time someone had suggested he get a general contractor's license. Mark was released two years early from prison for good behavior and had to completely start his life over, at the age of 32. His lawyer was able to keep the police from seizing his house after the drug raid because he still had tenants living in the house. Mark still had a lien on the house as well. Besides the property he almost lost while incarcerated, Mark had nothing. The good job with the bread company was gone, and he tried to get it back, to no avail. Fortunately, the police didn't confiscate his construction tools, and Mark was determined to live for Christ and stay out of trouble. Since the police confiscated his vehicles in the raid, Mark didn't have transportation anymore. Even though he had to walk everywhere he went, Mark made no excuses for his situation and worked with what he had.

Every morning Mark would get his 30 pound bag of tools and start walking to find work. After a month of walking with no work, he finally found a contractor that would give him a chance. The job could not have come at a better time since Mark had to find employment to meet his parole obligations. Many companies are hesitant to hire convicted felons, and Mark was rejected by eight construction companies before he got his break. You can never give up or lose your faith. Mark believes that what God has for him can't be taken away by anything or anyone. He had faith that God would provide him with a job, because he believed God would provide him with the things he needed to stay out of trouble.

The contractor who gave Mark his break started him off on a roof job. A month after being released from prison, he was working on his long-term plan of becoming a general contractor. The work was very demanding, and the hours were long. The asphalt shingles used in roofing can reach temperatures well over 100 degrees in the summer, and Mark worked an average of 14 hours a day. These circumstances did not bother Mark at all. He was willing to work hard in the short term to get what he wanted in the long term, and Mark was determined to start his own construction company. His work was impeccable, and his technical expertise was unmatched. The foreman on the roof job noticed the work Mark was doing and had empathy for his daily five-mile walk to work. The reason for this empathy was that the foreman was a convicted felon himself. He knew what Mark was going through and wanted to help him redeem himself. To help

Mark, the foreman sold him a 1972 Chevy pickup for $1,200. The foreman knew Mark didn't have all the money, so he let him make weekly payments of $100 until he paid off the truck.

This was the break Mark needed. Now, he could go out and find his own work. The next step he had to make was to save up enough money to get insured and bonded. The reason you have to get insured and bonded is that customers want to know they won't be held liable if a contractor gets hurt on a job. After a few months, he was able to save up enough money to pay off his truck and get insured and bonded. The one gift Mark has always had is the ability to talk to anyone. He got a business license, had some business cards and flyers made, and started his construction business. Since he was an outstanding roofer, Mark stuck with what he knew best and began to do roofing jobs.

Business was slow at first, but his ability to network eventually landed him work. On top of everything else, Mark found out that a young lady he had started dating when he got out of prison was pregnant. Now he had another responsibility besides himself to handle. He had never been married and didn't know anything about raising a child. The only thing he did know was that his child would want for nothing in his or her life. This only motivated him more to accomplish his goals. The only things Mark had working in his favor were his work ethic and his honest word. Establishing a good rapport with customers and keeping your word is essential in business. These attributes worked well for him.

According to Mark, "God gave me the wisdom to know that helping people and hustling for roof jobs was a lot better than hustling drugs, meeting crooks, and drug addicts." Mark's philosophy was to stay honest, and people would give him work. He's always been an honest person and never stole anything from anyone. This philosophy would take Mark very far in his business. He also believed that most drug dealers are not thieves and believe in hard work. Being able to talk to anyone and working hard are attributes Mark believes he developed when he was selling drugs. I am a strong believer that any negative situation can be changed into a positive one. This is one of those situations. Mark's favorite saying is, "I have never met a stranger, because I will talk to anyone!" Again, there is nothing wrong with the ambition and drive of illegal hustlers, but it is the target market, products, and services that need to change.

Mark's philosophy was the beginning of his competitive advantage. He strongly believes that you have to be honest and trustworthy in business, and Mark still tries to give his customers a good deal on their roofs. When a person would get an estimate from one of the big roofing companies, they would give the customers extremely high estimates. In many cases, a roof can cost well over $10,000. When a person would get an estimate from Mark, he would rarely charge a customer over $4,000 for the average roof. The only money he wanted was enough to cover his materials and make a 20% profit. When customers found out Mark was charging 60% less than his competitors, he literally had the neighbors of his customers chasing his truck down the street for his business.

How did they find out? The customers would brag to everyone in the neighborhood, including their friends and family, about the great job Mark did and how affordable he was. Not only did they pay 60% less, but the quality of the roofs was immaculate. Mark also gives a 10-year warranty on his work. Most of his competitors only give five-year warranties. The reason he offers a 10-year warranty is that there are some competitors who might offer a lower price on roofs, but Mark is able to differentiate himself from these competitors with quality as well. Other roofers know their roofs aren't going to last more than five years without a problem. When some customers choose to go with another roofer instead of Mark, they usually end up calling him back because the other roofer ended up doing a terrible job. Quality work will speak for itself every time. Mark never went to college and studied the business philosophy of TQM, but he implements it in every aspect of his business.

In his first year, Mark made approximately $15,000, but he made well over $70,000 in his second year of business. He also had a new baby daughter and bought a new Ford F-150 in his second year. By Mark's fourth year in business, he was making well over $100,000. I don't know about anyone else, but I would be more than willing to wait four years to make over $100,000.

If an individual is an illegal hustler and tried to get this type of money in the short term, they could end up doing an average of 10 years or more in prison. Instead of planning for the long term, an illegal hustler could end up giving 10 years or more of his or her life to a correctional facility. Including Mark's prison sentence, it took him eight years to make $100,000. Even though he went to prison, he changed his life and now is a millionaire. If an individual works hard and stays legit, he or she could cut the time it took Mark to make $100,000 in half.

The most shocking part of Mark's strategy is the fact that he does not advertise! He doesn't even have a listing in the phone book. All of the business he gets is from referrals. He strongly believes that if you give customers the best deal, be honest, and establish a rapport with them, they will refer you to other customers. According to Mark, he built his business from people trusting him and giving him referrals for other customers. When I rode with him, he used to get a significant amount of calls from the relatives and friends of people he had helped out.

Many of Mark's customers can't afford a roof at all. Either he sets up a payment plan with them, or he stops their roof from leaking if they have no money. The mission of his company is to help as many people as possible and build a relation with customers, built on trust. This strategy has worked for the past 20 years, and Mark's competitors cannot duplicate or imitate his success. The reason for this is that most roofers have to spend a substantial amount of money on advertising and have no room to give customers a break. With Mark eliminating the need to market, the savings of not advertising are passed down to the customer. Mark worked by himself the first couple of years. By his fifth year, Mark had a five-man crew and was looking into the requirements for becoming a general contractor.

Being a general contractor is so lucrative because you are able to subcontract different jobs of a construction project such as painting, electrical, plumbing, and other jobs to other contractors. In other words, you are able to make a profit off the work others are doing. It's very expensive to become a general contractor. Mark stated he has spent approximately $18,000 to get his general contractor's license, and the process took him almost a year to complete. The majority of the money was spent on classes, licenses, liability insurance, and certifications. After he obtained his general contractor's license, he opened up a full construction company and bought several pieces of heavy-duty equipment. The equipment he purchased enabled his company to bid on new construction projects for residential and commercial property. He is currently looking into building a set of condominiums on some land he owns.

On top of generating good revenue from his construction projects, he is still one of the best roofers in the state of Tennessee. His company is able to travel to different states and help rebuild neighborhoods after natural disasters, such as hurricanes and tornados. Mark's company was one of the first construction companies to arrive in New Orleans to help rebuild the city after the devastation of Hurricane Katrina. Even though Mark lost money in New Orleans when he went down there to help the hurricane victims, he was happy to help the people of New Orleans get back on their feet. The losses Mark took on in New Orleans balanced out, because his business made record profits from an active weather season in Tennessee and other parts of the south. From 2006 to 2008, Mark's company made over $12 million.

At this point, I was curious about how Mark was able to make this kind of money. My goal was to find out how he made $100,000, now we were discussing millions. I noticed that his sales went up when there was a series of bad weather conditions. Mark has been able to become the primary contractor for many insurance companies. I recall an incident when my truck was in a traffic accident. When I had my wreck, my insurance company immediately responded and referred me to a body shop. The one thing that I noticed is that the body shop didn't have to advertise for business, because the insurance company was bringing them clients. I asked Mark did he have a similar arrangement with any insurance companies. Mark confirmed that he did have several insurance companies referring customers to him. He went on to explain that only the best contractors are able to get insurance referrals, and he had to be willing to accept the price that insurance companies set.

Anytime there is a major storm, Mark's phone explodes with calls from insurance companies needing his services. Most of the damage that occurs from severe storms affects the roof of a home. Insurance companies want a contractor that will repair or replace the roof for the lowest cost and the highest quality. That is when Mark comes in with his three roofing crews. Not only are his roofing crews very professional and good, but they are extremely fast as well. When his company replaced my roof, they were able to tear off the old roof and install the new one in one day. After they replaced my roof, I didn't find an old shingle or a single nail anywhere on the ground. It was like they were never there, but I had a brand new roof as evidence that they were. This type of quality and service will make you want to tell someone how good of a job Mark does. I witnessed it myself and was more than willing to tell my family and friends. Mark emphasized that being the lowest bidder is just one part of the equation. You have to have the quality in your work along with a fair price.

Since Mark was making so much money, I knew he must have had some investments to maintain his wealth. The first thing that came to mind was stocks and bonds. I was shocked to find out that Mark does not invest in the stock market at all. Even though the housing market was in a serious slump, Mark still invested in real estate. He has been investing in real estate so long that falling prices in the market does not scare him away at all. By Mark being so close to the industry, he is able to find foreclosures and dilapidated properties which he remodels and flips. The key to Mark's strategy is to sell real estate under the market value. According to Mark, one of the biggest myths in the real estate market right now is that Americans are not buying homes. People are still buying real estate, especially first-time home buyers. The first-time home buyer market is the one that Mark has targeted, and business is good, to say the least. When Mark is unable to sell a house right away, he simply rents the property until he is able to sell it. He also offers a lease-purchase option where customers can simply rent-to-own his properties. Mark also invests the traditional way, by simply putting his money in a savings account and not spending it. Even though the returns are not very high, his money is safe and waiting for him anytime he's ready for it.

Mark is very active in the community when it comes to giving back. He often gives enormous discounts to seniors, churches, and other organizations in need of his services. In many cases he offers his services for free. One year, he even took his company to Argentina for a few months to build churches for the poor. Mark kept stressing the fact that you have to give back to people to get anything in return. The two-year period that his company made $12 million was the period in which he gave the most to charity as well. You often hear about people giving their money to charities, but you don't hear about people giving their time. Mark spends a lot of his time helping the disenfranchised. I can't help but think that his success is a direct blessing of his giving.

I asked Mark what the immediate future holds for his company. He told me that he plans to become a multi-millionaire in the next two years. The one thing he has done to meet this long-term objectives is delegate more of his authority to a new project manager he has hired. His new manager, John, is a subcontractor with a record of quality and getting the job done. In the past Mark had to micromanage many of his crews to ensure the job was done to his standards. The addition of John allows him to get out in the community and meet more people. By freeing up his time, he is able to give more estimates and has seen a 40% increase in sales since hiring the new project manager. I will definitely continue to track the progress of Mark's business and share my findings in an effort to help others pursue their dreams.

After evaluating Mark's case, I noticed he was using several keys of knowledge in his daily operations. The most obvious key of knowledge he was using was networking. Even though his networking skills began with his drug dealing activities, it culminated into him taking care of his customers and motivating them to find other customers for his business. This type of customer relationship can not be created overnight, and it takes time to build the kind of trust Mark has in his target market. To be effective at networking, you must be a great communicator. This doesn't mean that you have to be a great public speaker or very articulate, but it does mean that you have to expose yourself to your target market or anyone who comes across your path. You simply have to be willing to open up your mouth and talk to people.

I also noticed a great deal of leadership in Mark's operations. He led by example with his work ethic and expected everyone in his organization to do the same. Whenever you meet Mark, he's full of life, motivated and willing to listen and help others. Everyone in Mark's organization is willing to do whatever he asks of them. From Mark's account of his success, it's very obvious that he wasn't born a leader, but developed his leadership skills over the years. Many of his leadership skills developed from the trials and tribulations he has encountered.

Another key of knowledge which Mark has mastered is the key of discipline. It would have been so easy for Mark to slide back into his old ways once he was released from prison, but he put his drug deals and drug usage behind him and saw the bigger picture. When you are use to making easy money, it is a hard habit to break. Everyone likes to have money and not struggle for everything they want. Sometimes the struggle helps to build character, and I believe that is what Mark's struggle did for him. It gave him the disciple he needed to eliminate bad habits and concentrate on the long-term goals that ultimately made him a millionaire.

Mark's dedication to God was definitely a key of knowledge he embraced. On several occasions, he has expressed to me that he would be dead or back in prison if it wasn't for him finding God in prison. According to Mark, finding God gave him a purpose in life to help others, and he feels he has been truly blessed because of his efforts to help people. I'm not trying to persuade anyone's beliefs, but I find it ironic that Mark made the most money in his life when he helped people the most. This can not be written off as coincidence. I am a true believer that you have to believe in something greater than yourself to reach your goals. Mark's belief in God has surely been a catalyst in his efforts to become a multi-millionaire. I don't know too many people who have served time in prison and reached the levels of success that Mark has.

Focus was another key of knowledge Mark tapped into for his success. I recall Mark telling me about his five-mile walk to work everyday carrying over 30 pounds of tools. Not only was his load heavy, but the elements of the sun in the summer and the cold in the winter would cause anyone to lose focus. Mark didn't focus on what he had lost but focused on what he wanted to gain. I imagine Mark's tunnel vision was impeccable when he was walking to work everyday. He told me a few of his so called friends would honk their horns and laugh at him when they saw him walking. He couldn't recount too many occasions when someone would offer him a ride. Like Mark, you have to be willing to put your pride to the side to get the things you want out of life.

Faith was definitely one of Mark's key attributes. He had faith that God would bless him with the things he wanted out of life as long as he worked hard and stayed out of trouble. Mark didn't see a million-dollar business when he started contracting over 20 years ago, but he had faith that it was in God's plans. Not only was Mark's faith in God solid, but he had unbreakable faith in himself as well. He knew the skills and knowledge he possessed, and failure was definitely not an option for him. The confidence and faith he had in himself was noticed by customers, which strengthened their confidence and faith in Mark's ability to do a good job. This faith has resulted in Mark being one the biggest general contractors in Tennessee.

When Mark's old boss offered to sell him an old pickup truck, he saw this as an opportunity to rest his feet and build his business. Mark didn't focus on how old the truck was, and it wasn't the look Mark was use to having after owning a Corvette. He believed this opportunity would lead to a better vehicle and a better future in the long term. When it comes to putting pride to the side, Mark definitely did that when he purchased the old truck and didn't care how he looked riding in it. He laughs now at the times that the old truck would break down on the interstate, and he would still end up walking because his truck was so unreliable. Capitalizing on the opportunity to purchase the old truck is what led to Mark's ability to buy new Corvettes, trucks, motorcycles, and many other vehicles.

Education was very important in Mark's success. He didn't go to college, but he went to contractor's school, which enabled him to acquire his general contractor's license. Mark had a dream, and it took him disciplining himself to obtain the knowledge he needed to make that dream come true. He could have used the $18,000 to buy more materials or a new motorcycle, but he took the money and invested it in his education. From the looks of things, that $18,000 has paid for itself many times over in Mark's career. He also educated himself by listening to others and soaking up every bit of knowledge from people who had what he wanted. The education Mark received from listening to others was priceless.

I believe it takes an act of courage to deal with poverty, unemployment, and a criminal record. Mark had all three of these factors working against him when he was released from prison. He didn't let his circumstances dictate his life. Since he was 14, the one thing Mark feared the most was poverty. Mark had the courage to humble himself when he was broke and worked himself out of that situation. No one wanted to hire Mark after he got out of prison, especially with a drug conviction. Many people judge and scrutinize people who were once involved in drugs, and Mark was no exception to the judgment and scrutiny. When a contractor would turn him down, Mark would use the disappointment as motivation to find someone who was willing to take a chance on him. The courage Mark had enabled him to take the things he wanted through pure perseverance.

Let's re-examine the factors that are needed to create a competitive advantage in a target market:

1. Focusing on becoming the overall low-cost leader in an industry
2. Focusing on the creation and marketing of unique products for varied customer groups through differentiation

3. Focusing on having special appeal to one or more groups of consumer or industrial buyers, concentrating on their cost or differentiation concerns[6]

After analyzing the three factors and comparing them to Mark's organization, I believe he was able to capitalize on all three to create a competitive advantage in his target market. He has definitely made himself the low-cost leader in his industry. The reason he was able to do this is because he didn't have to advertise. While his competitors were spending thousands of dollars on TV commercials and radio ads, he advertised his business to one customer at a time. The money saved from the lack of advertising was passed down to customers, which helped him build customer relations and a name for his company. Mark's perspective was, "why make every dime you can off one customer, when you could make enough off one customer to be profitable and receive good referrals from satisfied ones?" Of course, there was not a substantial amount of money to be made in the short term with this strategy, but the strategy proved to be greatly effective in the long term. To this day, none of Mark's competitors have been able to beat his prices or his low operating costs.

When examining the second factor for a competitive advantage, the differentiation which Mark created to reach his target market was customer service. He made it his goal to become friends with everyone that hired him for work. According to Mark, "I built my business off of trust and referrals. If you can't trust someone, it's hard to be friends, and I was friends with all of my customers." From my experiences, I can't recall becoming friends with any business owner that I purchased a product or service from, except Mark. Most companies believe they are too big or too busy to establish a personal relationship with customers. This is why Mark's competition is scrambling to keep up with him. They don't practice "customer intimacy." This technique is honest and comes from the heart. Maybe that is the reason many business owners are reluctant to establish relationships with customers, because they are too busy trying to rob customers for everything they have. I have personally referred at least 10 customers to Mark, because he did such an excellent job on my home, and I wanted him to help someone the same way he helped me.

The third factor in establishing a competitive advantage states that you must have a special appeal to the customers to address their cost and differentiation concerns. Mark was able to create this special appeal with his low prices and high level of quality. Remember, customers seek you out when you are able to create this type of competitive advantage. There is a need in the target market that needs to be fulfilled. This is what happened in Mark's case when it came to dealing with insurance companies. Insurance companies have found out that Mark offers the best quality at the lowest price and use him exclusively in many cases. Like I stated before, only the best contractors are used by insurance companies. If Mark did not go out and sell another construction job, he knows he would be in good shape because of his insurance referrals.

According to Michael Porter, a company only needs to incorporate one of the factors for creating a competitive advantage to be successful. In Mark's case, he was able to incorporate all three factors for creating a competitive advantage. This is probably one of the reasons he is a millionaire and close to being a multi-millionaire. My purpose was to find out how he was able to make $100,000. Thanks to Mark, I was able to get that information plus a lot more. After analyzing Mark's case, I find it hard for anyone to have excuses why they cannot be successful. This man gave one year of his life to a state penitentiary and was still able to become a millionaire. Do you still have any excuses for not being successful after reading Mark's case?

The moral of Mark's story is to stop making excuses and accomplish the goals you have set for yourself by any means necessary, as long as it's legal. I know plenty of people who were released from prison, and they were back in prison within a year. Mark had started a company and turned a profit in his first year after being released from prison. This case study clearly showed that a person can make mistakes in the short term and completely redeem themselves in the long term. No one in this world is perfect, and a person who has been incarcerated is no different and deserves a second chance. Mark did not let the label that society had placed on him define who he was as a person, and he definitely did not let it stop him from accomplishing his goals. It takes dedication, drive, and courage for you to never give up and be able to turn a negative situation into a positive one.

NOTES:

Glen Rhodes, Supervisor at Insight Communications

Member of the hip-hop group Code Red

5 FROM CABLE TO CASH: THE SALESMAN

I am no stranger to hard times. When I was laid off in 2009, it was one of the most challenging events I had ever faced in my life. Even though I was able to start my own company right after I was laid off, my subcontracting business began to slow down in the winter months. Once again I was back in the hole, but I was determined to find another way to hustle. My hustling adventures landed me in Louisville, Kentucky working for Insight Communications. Insight is one of the largest providers of cable, telephone, and internet services in the country. Two of my friends worked there, and I asked them if they could help me get a position at the company. My guys said they had connections to make it happen, so I hit the road ready for my next hustle. My friend Glen was a door-to-door salesman for Insight, and my friend Mike was a customer-service representative for the company. My goal was to work in Louisville for a steady paycheck until I found work in Nashville. Considering that Glen worked outdoors and Mike worked indoors, I wanted a position in customer service. That was not meant to be.

The only position that was open at Insight was for a sales representative. I even had the audacity to tell my friend Mike with laughter in my voice, "there is no way I'm going to be a door-to-door salesman and get doors slammed in my face all day!" My friend Mike began to laugh and told me, "you might want to reconsider that decision once you find out how much they make." Once I found out how much an average sales rep at Insight made, I wasn't laughing anymore. The average sales rep at Insight made $70,000 a year, but my friend Glen was not the average salesman. He was making $100,000 a year selling cable door-to-door, and he had only been with the company for three years! Not only was Glen a successful salesman, but he also made a decent amount of money from being an independent hip-hop artist. This was the point at which I decided to stop laughing, shut up, and listen to what Glen had to say. Glen told me that I would get a base pay of $1,000 every two weeks until I was out of training, and training lasted for two months. I didn't hesitate to jump on the offer and worked for Insight for two months, until I got my position with the EEOC. In those two months I learned a great deal about sales, customer service, and myself. I made over $5,000 in that short period and discovered that the sales industry can lead to substantial wealth. A few months later Glen and I had a chance to sit down and discuss the aspects of selling and the music industry.

The first thing that caught me off guard about Glen was the fact he was very educated. I knew him by "Manfred," which is his stage name. Manfred is a lyrical genius who can make many words in the dictionary rhyme and make sense. When it comes to the ladies, Manfred has never found one he could not charm with his words and have their heart right where he wanted it. Manfred is a jokester who never takes anything serious and is always ready to party. At the same time, I really did not know how serious he was about hustling. Glen was a graduate of the University of Kentucky with a Bachelor's degree in Broadcast Journalism. You would think that with all of his talent and education he hasn't struggled one day in his life, but this wasn't the case. Glen told me that reality hit him directly in his face when he graduated college. Even though he wanted to be an anchor in his hometown of Louisville, Kentucky, none of the local channels wanted to give him a chance. The positions he did find in journalism were not paying enough to make ends meet and would never get him in front of a camera. Even though he found opportunities in other cities, he did not want to leave the city of Louisville.

According to Glen, he was not happy with his quality of life. He managed to find a job as a server at a chain restaurant making minimum wage and earning mediocre tips. The job was barely enough for him to pay rent and put gas in his car. Shortly after starting the serving job, he found out that his girlfriend at the time was pregnant. Glen knew that there was no way he could support himself and a child off the money he was making. A change had to come. He discovered this change in the sales industry. The sale of goods and services is a multi-billion dollar industry in the United States, and someone has to be the middleman between buyers and sellers of those goods and services. This is when salespeople come into the picture. Glen got his first major break into sales as a sales representative for AT&T. The job could not have come at a better time. His girlfriend had just had their child, and the job as a server couldn't even buy diapers for a week.

Glen discovered the sales position online and was hired almost immediately after applying. The company Glen worked for was a subsidiary for AT&T and sold telecommunications equipment to other businesses. Business-to-business sales is a very strong industry and has one of the highest commissions for sales reps. Glen was paid weekly, and net pay after taxes was over $1,000. The main factor that attracted Glen to sales was the ability to make an enormous amount of money in a short period of time. I asked Glen if his education played a significant role in his ability to get the job, and how much education did a person need to be a sales rep? His answer was very surprising.

According to Glen, "you don't have to have any education to be honest with you. There are people with GEDs or haven't even graduated high school working sales positions [sic]." I still stand by my belief that it should be mandatory for everyone to have at least a GED. My belief is that it's not about receiving a piece of paper, but it's about having concrete evidence of a person's ability to learn. Companies will still use education as an excuse to discriminate against individuals and not give them a job. Education is still a powerful weapon in Corporate America, and you have to always stay armed for battle. The only skills required to be a sales rep are strong communication skills, a high level of professionalism, the ability to learn quickly, and the ability to be a self-motivator. That is it. Glen went from making minimum wage to making over $1,000 per week, in only three weeks. The stress of not being able to provide for his child vanished almost overnight, and money problems were nonexistent at that point. He stated, "I went from making no money to more money I knew what to do with it [sic]." Glen had never experienced this type of fortune in his life.

Now, make no mistake about it. Glen didn't start off making $1,000 weekly because he was O.K. as a salesman, but he made that kind of money because he is a real hustler and constantly stayed on the road grinding it out. If you are not willing to get the door slammed in your face and get told "no" 50 times in a row, then sales is not for you. Sales requires a person to set goals and stop at nothing to achieve them. I have often heard Glen state that there were many nights he refused to go home until he had made a sale. You have to be ferocious in your efforts to attack the target market, but you also have to be gentle and persuasive enough to make the sale. A good salesperson can be characterized as a genius when it comes to communicating with customers.

One of the first things Glen noticed about sales was the enthusiastic atmosphere of the workplace. Everyone on the team was highly motivated and running around giving each other high fives all the time. He also liked the rewards systems that were in place. His base pay was netting him $400, but the bonuses would increase his pay to over $1,000. The primary motivator in sales is money. There is a significant amount of money to be made when a salesperson is good, but a person who can't sell will find themselves looking for another job real soon. The only thing Glen didn't like about his position was the level of freedom he was given. He had to meet a strict quota and could not deviate from the sales protocol in place. If he wanted to take lunch, it had to be taken on his assigned route. After working for the AT&T subsidiary for a year, Glen decided to look for other opportunities in sales.

He discovered a local waste company in Louisville called Ecotech. The company didn't have a quota system for sales, and the product pretty much sold itself to customers. Glen would go to a business offering to save them 40% on their waste disposal, and the customers would change waste companies immediately. The competitive advantage of smaller waste companies is their ability to lower their overhead by having less employees and cheaper equipment. Ecotech is an environmental-friendly company, so it also lowers costs by being more efficient and recycling. Glen was still getting paid weekly and was his own boss in his target market. According to Glen, "It was the easiest sale I ever made. The work environment was real relaxed, and I didn't have any set hours or days." He would go out and work only two or three days the entire week, but each sale he would get made him $25. A sale only took him four minutes at the most to make, and he would work for only five hours a day and make $600. At the end of the week, Glen's net pay was $1,500.

One would think this would be the "Promised Land" for a salesperson, but Glen believed he needed to be more disciplined and have more structure in his career. In other words, he thought the job was too relaxed and would lead to him getting into too much trouble. At first I thought he was crazy for leaving a job with that type of freedom, which allowed him to make $1,500 a week. After I carefully analyzed the situation, I understood completely the reason he decided to resign from Ecotech. When a person becomes complacent and fails to challenge themselves, he or she fails to reach their full potential and wastes the talent God gave them. Glen knew he could make more money if he challenged himself, so he started working for Insight Communications as a sales rep. The Louisville sales team has led the company in sales for the past few years. Glen knew he could excel in this winning environment. He started off working in the single-dwelling unit (SDU) as a sales rep. The sales unit focused on residential customers and required sales reps to sell their services door-to-door. The benefits the company offered were incredible, and many of the top sales reps were making six-figure incomes.

Another key factor that led him to Insight was the company's focus on customer service. Glen believes that you have to have good intentions as a salesperson by not taking advantage of the customer. Many salespeople will attempt to get a sale by any means, even if it's unethical and ultimately robs the customer. That has never been Glen's approach. He believes that "If you can get to the door, be professional, communicate with people, and understand where they are coming from, then you can be successful in this business." It's a simple philosophy but harder to carry out than you think.

From my experience, some customers will not let you get a word out of your mouth before they are telling you, "I am not interested." If you keep talking, they will just simply slam the door in your face. This describes a typical day for a door-to-door salesperson. Only the best salespeople can get around these barriers in the sales industry. I have seen Glen in action when he led training when I worked for Insight. He has a keen understanding of the customers' needs and knows what they don't want. Not only does he know every excuse and way customers say no, but he also has several techniques for getting a person to say yes. The one thing Glen taught me in training was to listen very carefully for the needs customers want fulfilled. A good listener can pick up on these needs in a basic conversation with customers. They always want to know what you can do for them. Glen believes that "you have to give the customer some justice. Whether you're saving them money or not, sincerely know you're giving them a better product than they have." Glen's primary goal is to always meet or exceed the expectations of the customer. That is why he has been very successful as a salesperson, because he always delivers on the customer's wants and needs.

As mentioned earlier, Glen has only been with Insight for three years, but he is already a legend at the company. When he first started, Glen was given the $1,000 guarantee that was paid every two weeks until he sold over that amount. After taxes this pay was approximately $750. This was not acceptable to Glen, because he demanded more out of himself. He received only one guaranteed check before he exceeded the goal by making $2,500 in two weeks. After two months of working with Insight, he was making approximately $3,500 every two weeks. Glen's primary goal was to get better and better at his hustle. This allowed him to make more money and have a better quality of life. According to Glen, "the two things I really needed in life from this sales job were to make enough money to take care of my family and have enough time to spend with my family." I found this statement to be very powerful; his goals were realistic and humbling, but he was blessed well beyond his expectations.

In the short term Glen set a daily goal of getting four sales a day. Even though he was working six days a week, Glen was only working two or three hours a day. If you do the math, he was getting approximately 1.5 sales an hour while only working 18 hours a week. Glen believes much of his success in sales came from being self-motivated. He realized no one was going to train him better than himself. People can soak up as much knowledge as they want to get, but they won't be successful until they get out there and apply the knowledge for themselves. Trial and error is an intricate part of learning, and I believe failure comes before success. You should never be afraid to fail, because success will follow if you are able to capitalize on your mistakes.

Glen was able to capitalize on his mistakes and has become one of the top salespeople at Insight. In his first year Glen made approximately $75,000 selling cable door-to-door. By his second year he had his sales hustle mastered and made approximately $92,000. This was only the beginning for him. After two years Glen was promoted to a sales supervisor and has a sales team of seven people. He made well over $100,000 in his third year at Insight. With all of his success, I knew that Glen had to have faced some tough challenges to climb the corporate ladder.

Corporate America is a cut-throat environment in which to find success, and I wanted to know what challenges he had faced. The first challenge he faced was maintaining his professionalism in such a laid back environment. Even though he came to Insight for more structure, Insight still gives its employees a significant amount of freedom to get their jobs done. Glen had to constantly remind himself that he was there to make money and not friends. The more time he spent in the field meant he would get more money. The other major challenge that he had experienced in Corporate America came as no surprise to me. The second challenge was his skin color. According to Glen,

> I'm just going to be real. Being an African-American man, I got to do double what everybody else does; I got to do double what my comrade does. Not to make a racial issue out of it, but I got to do double what my Caucasian counterpart is doing to make sure I'm noticed. I'm going to do everything it takes; I'm going to be innovative. I'm going to work hand and hand with my boss. I'm going to always make sure he has his eye on me and sees the positive things that I'm doing. I want everybody to know that I'm the best at what I'm doing.

Glen's approach to his job is how everyone should approach a corporate hustle. This goes back to removing yourself from organizational politics. When you are the best, your work ethic will speak for itself. Not only does Glen want his superiors and peers to know he is the best, but he wants his subordinates to know he is the best as well. When I was with Insight, Glen always had a daily training session with his team. If someone on his team was not meeting their sales goals, he would work with them until their goals were met. Real leaders expect the same success out of their followers that they expect out of themselves.

One of Glen's long-term goals is to become a multi-dwelling unit (MDU) salesperson. MDU reps work approximately half the time a SDU rep does and make almost double the income. MDU reps focus on apartment buildings and condominiums for their sales. The advantage to working in this department is that sales come to you. The only thing you have to do is sit back and wait for the phone to ring. The building managers call the MDU reps when a new tenant moves into the building. The only thing the MDU rep has to do is hit a switch in the building, and the new tenant has cable. Glen has the opportunity of making close to $200,000 a year if he can get into this position. This would be a lateral move for him, but the pay is well worth it. From his perspective, "it's really not about moving up in the company and becoming a manager or vice president. I would love to do that one day, but it's about the money right now." Glen wants to focus on making a lot of money as fast as he can, so he can have time to spend with his family. Again, his goals were humble, but the outcome was always gargantuan.

After discussing Glen's daytime hustle, I wanted to explore his nighttime hustle, which was the music industry. Glen is a member of the hip-hop group Code Red which is part of the independent record label 502 Headz. The group and the label are based out of Louisville, Kentucky. I have a lot of ties to the group and company, because my good friend Mike started them while we were both in the Army. After being in existence for over 10 years, the company has released three CDs and several mix CDs. I am somewhat fascinated with independent record labels because of the hustle and money that is involved in the business. Glen started his career as an artist in 1999, and 502 Headz signed him almost immediately in 2000. Even though Glen and Code Red haven't reached the mainstream with their music, they do have a loyal following of approximately 50,000 fans nationwide. Their fan base is mostly located in the Midwest, but the movement is gaining ground. Contrary to popular belief, many artists make more on an independent label than they would on a big label. Independent labels have less overhead and can afford to pay their artists more money.

Glen makes an average of $20,000 a year as a member of Code Red. He stated that he has made as much as $40,000 in the past from other business ventures associated with the group. For an independent artist, I thought this was good money. How could one artist on the label make this type of money, and the group only has 50,000 fans? I found this to be very intriguing to say the least. According to Glen, "we had a lot of things going through MTV, ESPN, movies, sporting events, and pro teams that actually generated decent income in a very short period of time." He was even amazed that Code Red could do a theme song for the Chicago Bears or the NCAA tournament, and the organizations were willing to pay so much money for background music. Glen went on to explain that the group makes good money from performing at live shows, selling Code Red merchandise, and being featured on other artists' music projects.

The majority of money independent artists make is generated from performing at shows. If you have ever been to a Code Red performance or heard their music, you would understand why the group has a loyal following and is sought out by MTV and ESPN. The energy these guys have on stage is phenomenal, and you definitely feel like you get your money's worth when the show is over. Glen believes that you have to be a real hustler to be in the independent-record business. That is because all of your income and opportunities are dependent on the work you do. These guys don't have multi-million dollar record companies giving them six or seven-figure budgets to create a record. In the end, I think the hustle makes you stronger and more successful in the long run. There are three other members of Code Red, so the group has generated anywhere from $80,000-$160,000 a year. It comes as no surprise to me that the group generates this type of income, because the music is good. The quality is impeccable, and these guys pour their hearts and souls into everything they do. If you are out there trying to get signed to a big record label, you need to stop and reevaluate your situation. Start your own record company and sell your product straight out of the trunk of your car. It's time to cut out the middle man and control your own destiny.

As far as his long-term goals, Glen wants to keep pursuing success with his music career and keep making a six-figure income at Insight. He would love for one of his songs to be a #1 hit and make millions of dollars, but he's being patient in the short term until that happens. According to Glen, "I would like to quit doing sales and focus strictly on music, but the reality of it is that I have to have something supporting me while I wait on that dream to manifest. It will happen!" I asked Glen what he does as far as investing his money, and the answer was very simple. He saves it. I know this first hand, because the man drives a beat-up 1998 Toyota Camry. Even though the Camry is sore on the eyes, it gets him from point A to point B and makes him over $100,000 every year. He believes you have to learn how to discipline yourself and save money, before acquiring a lot of materialistic possessions. Glen went on to explain that you have to plan for the worst-case scenario to really have financial stability. If the tires on his car blew out, Glen would have no problem writing a check for $400 due to his financial security. He believes that many people don't realize the value of saving money. Having financial security is being able to keep five figures in your checking and savings accounts at all times. It's after you have acquired that type of wealth that Glen believes you should spend money on the finer things in life.

Glen might drive an old Camry, but his condominium is a totally different story. He has a flat-screen TV in almost every room, and he has a terrace view that overlooks a lakefront. His daughter's room also has a flat-screen TV, and she hasn't even started the 1st grade yet. Glen told me that he recently went to

Ashley Furniture and bought a dining room set for $1,500, and he didn't even blink when he paid for it in cash.

If you have been keeping track, Glen makes approximately $120,000 on average from multi-hustling and has a quality of life that many people would love to have. At this point, I wanted to know how Glen always seems to be in the right place at the right time. I see sales positions all the time, but he seems to always know which opportunities to take. Why was he so successful? Glen really humbled me with his answer. He stated with confidence, "when I make career changes or major decisions, I pray on it. My daughter's life is in my hands, and I have to pray on it. I trust that the Lord is always going to lead me in the right direction." I really wasn't expecting that answer from Glen, because I have never heard him talk about his faith or God. From my perspective, a person doesn't have to go to church, the mosque, or the synagogue everyday to have faith in God. For true believers, God resides in one place, and that place is the heart. I asked Glen what advice would he give to someone thinking about going into the sales industry. He gave me the following answer:

> You have to be self-motivated. Sales is no joke. It's a bridge of tests. The things you learn in sales are the things you apply to life everyday. Sales is about perseverance and learning how to handle rejection when people don't like you or want you. How do you handle that? The reason I'm so passionate about sales is because it's really a lesson in life. The way you treat a sale is the way you treat people in life. When you approach negativity or you are unsure of yourself, how do you react? Sales teaches you to respond with confidence, professionalism, and determination. You have to be yourself in this business.

When I finished studying Glen's case, I noticed many similarities between him and Mark. Both of these gentlemen were faced with difficult situations, but they didn't let their

96

current situations dictate who they were as people and where they wanted to go in life. Glen applied several keys of knowledge to his hustle, but the main ones that he really capitalized on were faith, opportunity, focus, and discipline. When an opportunity came Glen's way, he prayed on the situation and executed a game plan. I believe this is how life should be approached. You have to have faith that you are doing the right thing and seize an opportunity when it comes your way. For the longest I would turn my nose up at sales positions, until I went broke and had to step out of my comfort zone. If Glen had never taken the opportunity to work for AT&T, his career probably would not be as successful as it is now.

To be a good salesperson, you have to be focused. There will be days when you are knocking on doors in the cold, heat, rain, snow, and sleet, but you have to be focused on making that sale. It took me three months to finally get Glen to sit down and conduct the interview. If Glen is not taking care of his daughter or in the studio, he's in the target market with his team making sales. He is constantly focused on the mission at hand, and that is why he has been so successful as a salesperson and musician. I have seen Glen perform in front of an audience no larger than 30 people, but he gave a performance like it was a packed arena. These days it's not hard to sell out a Code Red event in the Midwest. Glen and Code Red never focused on how many zeros were behind a check they received for performing. They were just focused on the next show and making it better. Whether it's the music industry or sales, it's almost impossible to make Glen lose focus when he's in the zone.

When a person is making the kind of money Glen has, it's easy to spend money on materialistic things and end up broke. Glen has had the discipline to know that just because he's making a six-figure income this year, doesn't mean he will be making six figures in the future. Glen's savings goal is to have $100,000 on standby at all times. This type of savings takes a discipline many people simply don't have. To be honest, I didn't have that type of discipline when I was making $60,000 annually. It took me losing my job, going through hard times, and really knowing the value of a dollar. Now, I am disciplined enough to know that the finer things in life will come with a little patience, hard work, and discipline.

Glen was even willing to leave a company that let him do whatever he wanted to gain the structure and discipline he knew he was lacking. A lack of discipline can lead to a person being complacent with a bad situation. If you are broke, why are you eating out everyday? If you don't own a home, why would you go out and buy a brand new car? These are things people do when they don't have the discipline to save their money and focus on long-term goals. The next time you think about purchasing a car, remember Glen and his 1998 Toyota Camry. He makes over $100,000 a year and doesn't have a car payment. Discipline is what keeps Glen wealthy while others are making the same type of money but living check to check.

The competitive advantage that most applied in Glen's case was the third factor: Focusing on having special appeal to one or more groups of consumers or industrial buyers, concentrating on their cost or differentiation concerns.[6] Glen stated that it wasn't about how much the product cost but the quality of the product that you are trying to sell the customer. Even though Glen doesn't own Insight, he owns his situation which is much more valuable. Insight is Glen's corporate customer, and his professionalism played a significant role in him getting his position. Now he is in a position where climbing the corporate ladder is irrelevant. If you were making $100,000 a year, would you really care about being a vice president in the company? I would rather have my special appeal to customers rather than deal with organizational politics. The same competitive advantage exists in his music career as well. Glen and Code Red have a loyal following, and the deals they have with MTV, ESPN, and the NFL make sure the royalty checks keep coming. I don't know too many independent artists who have these types of opportunities, and Code Red's success can't be easily duplicated.

Glen, Manfred, or whatever you want to call him is a complex, intelligent, wealthy, and humble man. He knows what his goals are, and he will stop at nothing to accomplish them. That is the type of dedication a person needs to be successful and never want for anything out of life. Either a person is busy making things happen or busy making excuses why things are not happening. You have to ask yourself which situation best describes you. I believe there is a salesperson that lives in all of us. What are you selling, and who is your target market? From Glen's perspective he is selling his professionalism and expertise, and his target market is anyone with money that is ready to spend it. Glen is a true multi-hustler, and his level of knowledge and determination can't be denied.

Mignon Francois, Owner of The Cupcake Collection

6 FROM FLOUR TO A FORTUNE: THE CUPCAKE LADY

The final case study definitely brings together the critical points of the ten keys of knowledge. Mignon Francois, owner of The Cupcake Collection, was able to create a booming business with no debt, but she overcame several challenges that would have broken the average person. Unlike the other case studies, Mignon's approach to business was very unorthodox and a means for survival. When I first met Mignon, she was giving a speech at a Black History Month program about the empowerment of minorities in business. The other speakers at the program gave the typical speech about being a business owner and what they did to become successful.

Mignon's speech was about her business, but her message was unlike any I had ever heard. From the beginning of her speech, until the end, Mignon focused on the power of faith and what faith had done in her life. She spoke with a real presence and had a smile on her face the entire time. By the time she had finished her speech, several women in the audience had tears streaming down their faces; and I even noticed a couple of men holding back tears. For the people who weren't crying, their mouths were hanging wide open from pure amazement. Everyone was standing on their feet giving her a standing ovation. That is how powerful and moving the speech was. Before I heard her speech, I thought my faith was strong and could get me through anything. After hearing her speech, I truly knew what the meaning of faith was.

I had the opportunity to sit down with Mignon for an exclusive interview. The day I conducted the interview was absolutely perfect. I went to Mignon's bakery as soon as I left my daytime hustle. It was a nice, sunny 72 degrees outside, and I could smell the enticing aroma coming from the bakery as soon as I opened my truck door. I parked about a half block away from the bakery, and the aroma of the cupcakes was still driving me crazy! The last time I smelled something so wonderful was over 20 years ago in my late grandmother's kitchen. I had a serious case of nostalgia at this point. When I went inside the bakery, I saw Mignon hard at work making cupcakes in the back. I finally got her attention, and she gave me a warm smile and told me to have a seat on the patio where I was going to conduct the interview. This gave me a chance to observe how intense the demand was for these incredible cupcakes. The line of customers at the bakery was running out of the door as usual, and many of the customers had to stop and talk to Mignon before they left. Mignon has established a great rapport with most of her regular customers. From what I noticed, Mignon treated her customers like family. The word was out on The Cupcake Collection. Everybody wanted to get their hands on one of Mignon's delicious cupcakes. I've even heard people refer to them as "a little bite of heaven." Mignon finally caught a break from baking cupcakes and sat down with me to give the interview.

Since I had heard some of the trials and tribulations of her story from the speech she gave, the first thing I wanted to know about Mignon was when her struggle began. According to Mignon, her struggle began 16 years ago when she was a newlywed. She and her husband Xavier were like the average middle-class family; they were living way above their means trying to keep up with the American dream. They were worried about the material possessions other people had and the things they thought were needed to be considered successful. Education is one of things Mignon believed she needed to be successful. Mignon is a very intelligent woman and has a dual bachelor's degree in mass media and psychology. Even though she was well educated, she was still struggling and hadn't found her ultimate calling in life. Mignon and Xavier are true adventurists and risk takers. In the beginning of their marriage, they made a pact with each other to move to another city every five years. This is something that she learned from her mother. When Mignon was growing up, her mother would relocate to another city every five years for new opportunity. Her mother was a strong believer that people learn about different cultures and backgrounds when they are willing to explore new adventures. This has made Mignon a very diverse individual and gave her the ability to adapt to any situation. Mignon currently lives in Nashville, Tennessee but originated from New Orleans, Louisiana. She and her family moved to Nashville after her husband accepted a new job in the city.

As soon as Mignon and her family moved to Nashville, Xavier found out that the company he was going to work for decided to move the position to another state. On top of this, the company did not have another position for Xavier to fill. This was devastating to the family, especially since Mignon was out of work as well. To make ends meet, Xavier tried to find work wherever he could. He found work remodeling homes, but the work wasn't steady. As she watched her husband work extremely hard to put food on the table, Mignon literally saw death on her husband's face. He would leave home early in the morning before sunrise and wouldn't return home until after sunset. The stress Xavier was under was tremendous. All of his efforts were not enough to provide for six children and a wife. Mignon knew her family could not continue like this, so she asked God for guidance.

Her faith in God has always been strong, and the financial storm her family was facing was not about to break it. Mignon decided it was time for her to break her family from the oppression of debt and despair, and she had faith that God would give her the wisdom to do so. Mignon is a loyal follower of the teachings of Dave Ramsey. She would listen to his show about people becoming debt free by taking charge of their situations and creating wealth for themselves. The strongest message she received from the show was being able to sell.

People were calling the show with tears of joy after becoming debt free. Mignon learned from the show that people were doing simple things like having yard sales to get out of debt. She would constantly listen to Dave expressing the importance of selling, but Mignon didn't have a clue what to sell in this new city. This is when she asked God with boldness to give her a plan, and her prayers were definitely answered. According to Mignon, "I learned that God cannot stand a wimp! It tells you that in the Bible, and we are supposed to be strong and courageous."

Her awakening came late at night when she was watching a fundraiser on the PBS Channel. A gentleman was on the channel raising money, and the first thing she heard him say was "the morning breeze has something to tell you. Do not go back to sleep." The first thing she thought was, "what is this foolishness this man is talking about?" She continued to listen and began to understand the message. Mignon is a strong believer that God is constantly talking to us, and He talks to us through our guts. She doesn't believe that the message comes to our minds or in our ears, but the message from God goes deep into our souls and can be felt deep in our bodies. This is the feeling Mignon had when she heard the gentleman make the statement. She continued to listen to the gentleman and learned that God talks to us in the quietness of the morning.

Mignon believes this quietness comes in the early morning hours when most people are asleep. Before she heard this message, she would wake up at approximately 3:15am every morning to use the bathroom and go back to sleep. After hearing the gentleman's message, she realized this was her time to talk to God and wouldn't go back to sleep after her 3:15am bathroom break. At first she would struggle with getting up at 3:15am every morning and not going back to sleep, but the routine got easier after awhile. This is when things started to happen in Mignon's life. She heard God in a way that she hadn't heard Him before, and His voice to her was very clear and was felt in her soul. The message she received from God was to walk in boldness and be courageous for whatever she asked of Him.

Mignon is quick to admit that she knew nothing about baking before she began her spiritual journey. The talent of baking actually came from her two daughters, Brittany and Lauren, who were 11 and 16 years old at the time. One evening Mignon was in the kitchen with her daughters while they were baking cupcakes. Mignon knew her daughters could bake, but she didn't have a clue they could bake from scratch. After Brittany and Lauren had baked the cupcakes they were going to take to school the next day, Mignon decided to try one. To Mignon's surprise, the cupcakes were incredible. She had to ask the girls, "what did you two put in these cupcakes?" The daughters replied, "a little of this and a little of that." At that very moment, Mignon knew that God wanted her to start baking cupcakes. According to Mignon, the vision was so clear that it could not be ignored. She continued to pray and ask for guidance since she didn't have a clue about baking. For the next few months, Mignon experimented and created over 18 delicious flavors of cupcakes. The recipes were simple, and the ingredients were fresh.

At first Mignon sold cupcakes out of her home. She knew the vision was much bigger than her kitchen, and more space was needed. The quest for a building had begun. Mignon looked everywhere before she found a rundown home in the area of Germantown. The Germantown neighborhood in Nashville is one of the most prestige areas in the city. The neighborhood was once one of the biggest crime areas in the city until it was redeveloped. Now, homes start at around $400,000 in Germantown. Mignon was very blessed to find a home in this area, but she knew she could not afford it. The seller was asking for $10,000 down, and the house had to be completely restored before a bank would even place a mortgage on it. This did not deter Mignon. She knew the vision she had for her cupcake bakery was meant for this house. Once again, Mignon decided to go to God in boldness to get this house. Mignon went to God with a tremendous amount of courage with the following prayer:

> God, I want you to give me this house which they want $10,000 down; I want you to bless me with living in the house rent and mortgage free for a year; I want to live there rent and mortgage free, so I can work on the house; I want you to bless me to do this with no money down; and I want the person selling the house to say yes to these terms.

At this point, I was completely astonished by Mignon's boldness and faith in God. Who was this woman to go to God with such courage and expected Him to answer her prayer? I don't know too many people who would go to God with this type of faith and courage, including myself. After Mignon revealed to me what God did for her after this prayer, my personal faith and courage were strengthened. At first Mignon was faced with doubt from everyone including her husband. Xavier thought the owner of the house would never agree to the terms Mignon wanted, but she had undying faith that the owner of the house would agree to the terms. When Mignon presented the offer to the homeowner, he told her "you must be crazy if you think I'm going to agree to those terms! This is Germantown. I get offers on this property all the time."

Even though Mignon's plan seemed bleak at the time, she didn't give up on the property. Something told her to be patient and present the offer to the homeowner again. She waited about three months and offered the homeowner the same deal. This time he was willing to negotiate. This is the same man who told Mignon she must be crazy to think he would agree to the terms she set. Not only did Mignon get the property under her terms, but the homeowner paid the property taxes for a year and offered her husband an opportunity to work on other properties he owned. This was done to compensate the homeowner for the

Francois' living in the house, free for a year. Now the Francois' had the property with no money down and no payments for an entire year. The homeowner did not have a loan on the property, so he could do whatever he wanted to do with the property. In other words, the deal he made with the Francois' was not hurting him at all.

Mignon's entire family worked on the house, including her three-year-old son. Can you imagine seeing a little boy with a little tool belt and hammer trying to help his family get their house in order? The dedication that the Francois' had to this house was impeccable. The house was in complete shambles when the family began to work on it. The plaster walls were falling off the wooden beams; the old and stained carpet was mildewed and molded; windows were broken out; and trash was everywhere. After a week of working in the house, the Francois' had torn out all of the bad plaster, ripped up the bad carpet, replaced broken windows, and removed all of the trash. Since Xavier was working on other properties for the homeowner, he would take scrap materials from those jobs and use them on Mignon's project. This was a clear example of a person putting their pride to the side and doing what needed to be done. Using the scrap materials from other jobs saved the Francois' a great deal of money which they did not have anyway.

After the first week of work, the homeowner came by to check on the progress. He was absolutely shocked by how much work the Francois' had done to the house. The first thing he asked Mignon was "why would you work like this?" He asked her this because the Francois' had exceeded the requirements to get the house back in shape. The family was definitely walking by faith and not by sight. They did not care about the condition the house was in or how bad it smelled, but they were focused on the vision that Mignon had for the property. The Francois' had friends and caring people in the neighborhood that would come by and lend a helping hand. People would even bring by food and water for the hard-working family. After the first week, the homeowner was so impressed by the Francois' that he gave them $2,000 for their hard work. This was definitely a blessing since the family had no income and used every dime they did get to fix up the house. According to Mignon, "you can ask God for whatever you want, and he will give it to you. I asked God for the bakery and He gave it to me." Mignon continued to reiterate the fact that you cannot go to God like a wimp. You have to go to Him with boldness and courage when you ask Him for the things you want. According to the Scripture, the faith of a mustard seed can move mountains. I believe Mignon's faith moved several mountains of adversity out of her way and was the primary source of her success.

Mignon made a promise to God that if He made the bakery a success, she would tell anyone who would listen about who He is; what her family had been through; what He had done for her family; and where their undying faith was taking them. She made these promises while she was in the middle of her struggle. At this point, the Francois' were doing the best with what they had. According to Mignon, she learned how to feed six children, her husband, and herself with $5 a long time ago. The family was eating a great deal of Ramen noodles and other inexpensive meals to survive. A meal that included meat was a luxury for the Francois' and only happened maybe once a month. This was the sacrifice they were willing to make to see their dreams come true. I normally spend at least $5 every time I eat! Can you imagine feeding eight people with $5? Before Mignon opened the bakery, she was baking cupcakes for people just to put food on the table.

After a year of hard work, Mignon was able to get a mortgage on the house and made plans to open the bakery. To save money, the family also moved into the home. The house was big enough to have a separate living area and plenty of room for a bakery. It took Mignon two years to finally get the bakery open. The first year of business was tough. She opened the bakery with a dorm-sized refrigerator and kitchen-aid mixer for making cupcakes. When the health department came through for the initial inspection, they had no problem with the refrigerator. As long as it could keep the products at the required temperature, it was approved for business. Even though Mignon needed additional equipment and supplies for operations to be fully functional, she worked with what she had.

The first day the bakery opened was almost the last day. Moments before Mignon opened the door to the bakery for the first time, she noticed the electric company coming down the street and about to turn into the alley behind the bakery. When the Nashville Electric Service (NES) truck is out, someone's electric service is about to get disconnected. Mignon already knew the truck was coming for their house. Xavier hurried up and got to the alley where the truck was. He explained to the NES driver that his wife was opening up her business at that very moment and asked him not to cut the electricity off. The driver gave them an additional week to come up with the money. On top of that situation, the Francois' had received an auction date on their property because it was in foreclosure. The date was set for the following week. Now they had to come up with the money to pay the electric bill and get their home out of foreclosure. Mignon made just enough money in that first week to pay the electric bill and get their home out of foreclosure. She believed it was the grace of God that helped her overcome those obstacles. According to Mignon, "God always honors your struggle. The richest people in the world always started off as the poorest people in the world."

Three months after opening, Mignon's business was definitely growing. Their first Valentine's Day, The Cupcake Collection had a line out the door. One of the neighbors came by to order cupcakes and noticed the tiny mixer Mignon was using to make the mouth-watering desserts. He asked Mignon "that's all you have? You have a line out the door, and that's what you're using to make the cupcakes?" She told the neighbor "you know you got to do what you got to do." He told her to come see him at the end of the day. The neighbor owned a pasta shop and had a gargantuan commercial-grade mixer. The mixer was worth well over $1,500. The circumference of the mixer was the size of tractor-trailer tire. The neighbor wanted $600 for the mixer. He owned it for a while and didn't need it anymore. After thinking about it for a moment, the neighbor then offered the mixer to Mignon for $200. Mignon was so grateful for the neighbor's generosity that she expediently wrote a check for $200 and gave it to the man. She had just met the neighbor two days prior.

The following week, Mignon noticed an industrial-size refrigerator for sale on Craig's list. The owners were selling it for $400. The refrigerator would normally cost approximately $3,000, but the sellers were closing down their business and didn't need it anymore. Once again, she quickly wrote a check and purchased the refrigerator. Mignon kept capitalizing on opportunities like this one. She would go to the habitat-for-humanity thrift store to purchase items for remodeling their home and bakery. When you go into the bakery, there is a beautiful glass case that the cupcakes are in on display. Mignon actually got the glass for the case from an old school that was being remodeled. Xavier went to the job site and asked the contractors for the old glass, and the contractors were happy he was getting rid of it for them. The glass would easily cost $2,000 brand new. Her husband was able to find several good doors from the job site as well. If you do the math, Mignon was able to acquire $6,500 worth of materials and equipment for $600. This is the type of hustling that keeps entrepreneurs like Mignon in business when others fail. According to Mignon, "we didn't have any cash, but we had creativity." This creativity has taken The Cupcake Collection a long way.

Mignon has barely been in business for two years, and the bakery has already made well over $100,000 in sales. After being in business for two months, Mignon made approximately $3,500 in profits. Compared to having no income, this was big money for Mignon. She has even been able to purchase a delivery bus for getting cupcakes to customers throughout Nashville and the Middle Tennessee area. The cupcake bus also reflects the creativity of Mignon with beautiful colors and cupcakes painted on the bus, as a mural.

With the addition of the cupcake bus, she has been able to offer catering services for clients. Instead of traditional wedding cakes, many clients buy dozens of cupcakes stacked high for their wedding receptions. One of the favorite flavors demanded for catering is the white icing and cake creation called "the wedding cake." I have experienced the joy of eating a wedding cake, and it absolutely melts in your mouth with each bite. The catering service is in such high demand that there is a one year waiting list to have a wedding catered. Mignon even had to turn down catering jobs for weddings, because there are just too many of them!

The Cupcake Collection also serves the Clarksville, TN/Fort Campbell, KY area with cupcakes. Many active-duty military and retired personnel live in the area, and the cupcakes are in high demand. The cupcakes are selling so well in this area that customers are demanding a store be opened instead of having them delivered on the cupcake bus. The cupcake deliveries to the Clarksville/Fort Campbell area are outpacing sales in the original store. Mignon is currently making plans to open up a store in the area.

I asked Mignon what her long-term goals were when she started her business. Her answer was very surprising and humbling. She really didn't set long-term goals in the beginning. Her main goal was to be able to provide for her family. This was the ultimate goal for starting the business. According to Mignon, "I just wanted to make it! I wanted to be able to pay for my children to go on field trips. I wanted to have lights everyday and not worry about them getting shut off." Too often, her children would come home and the water would be cut off, or the lights would be cut off. Every time one of her children would ask if the lights or water was cut off again, it would break Mignon's heart. Mignon believes that no nine-year-old should know about adding water to the toilet to make it flush when the water would get cut off. These are the types of heartbreaks that her family had to endure until she put God first and started her business.

In the short term, Mignon did everything she could to sell more cupcakes. She would get up early in the morning, say her prayers, get her kids ready for school, and go straight into the kitchen to experiment with different recipes. Remember, Mignon could not bake before she started her business. The morning was the perfect time for her to educate herself on the aspects of baking. Mignon believes in the Chinese proverb that says, "a man who rises 365 days before dawn does not fail to make his family rich." When The Cupcake Collection first opened, it only had six different kinds of cupcakes. Thanks to Mignon's early morning experiments, the bakery now offers over 18 flavors of cupcakes. She is also in the process of creating more flavors.

Mignon's market research was a little unorthodox. She would find a construction site close to her bakery and take her trial cupcakes to the workers. The workers would give her their honest opinion, and she would know if she had a hit or a failure on her hands. As a matter of fact, anyone that was walking outside her bakery would often get the opportunity to try Mignon's cupcakes. If someone moved into the neighborhood, Mignon would be the first one to greet them with her cupcakes. The taste tests that she performed were nothing more than a basic survey. There are many ways to conduct a survey in a target market. Mignon simply found a way that worked for her business. She was able to find out which flavors customers liked and disliked. Some of the best flavors of cupcakes were created from Mignon's research, including banana nut cake, blackout (rich chocolate filled with chocolate mousse), caramel apple, carrot cake, coconut crème, cookies n' cream, key-lime pie, coconut, pineapple upside down, red velvet, strawberry, and many more.

Market research doesn't have to be expensive. It just needs to be creative.

Even though Mignon's business is thriving, the threat of competition still exists. There are several places in the Nashville area offering cupcakes, including local grocery stores. At the same time, no one can offer the type of customer service that Mignon delivers. In her mind there is no competition. This is the type of attitude a leader must have. You have to believe you are the best and constantly strive to be the best if you aren't. If a customer comes in and looks like they are having a bad day, Mignon will give them a cupcake. If a customer comes in and needs advice, Mignon will stop her work and help out the customer. Sometimes customers just need a hug, and she gives those out as well. There is nothing like establishing a personal relationship with your customers. When I asked Mignon what was the biggest advantage she has over her competitors, she stated her family was her competitive advantage. Several members of her family work in the bakery, and they really make you feel at home when you walk into the bakery.

Mignon has been very efficient with her marketing efforts as well. She simply started in her immediate radius telling people about her cupcakes, and people started coming into her bakery. Word-of-mouth traveled fast about The Cupcake Collection, and thousands of cupcakes are sold monthly due to one person telling another one about the bakery. In the beginning, her son would even stand on the sidewalk and tell everyone that passed by about the bakery. Now she gets so much free publicity that there is no need for a grand marketing campaign. Mignon has received several offers from media and TV to market her talents. Paula Dean from The Food Network has asked Mignon to be on her show, and the show "Cupcake Wars" wants her to make an appearance on an episode as well. She has even heard that Oprah Winfrey likes her cupcakes. Even though Mignon can't confirm this, it is very possible since Oprah has a lot of roots in the

Nashville area. When you have this type of buzz in the market, what is the use of advertising?

As far as investing, Mignon invests every extra dollar she has back into the business. The business is completely debt free, except for the mortgage on the building. At her current pace, Mignon will have it paid off in no time. Instead of buying the cupcake bus, she could have gone out and bought a new car. Mignon was smart enough to grow her business instead of her status in society. This type of discipline is needed to accomplish long-term goals. Even though she has had several offers to franchise her bakery, Mignon believes in taking one step at a time. She built her business from the ground up and is not ready to relinquish control of it through franchising. She knows that franchising could endanger the authenticity she has in her business, and that is the last thing she wants to do.

Mignon does a significant amount of charity work in the community. As I mentioned before, she gives away a good amount of cupcakes. When she hears about a death in the community, Mignon will often take the family of the deceased dozens of cupcakes. When one of the counselors at her children's former school died, she took the entire staff cupcakes. She also does several speaking events in the community, and her entire family is involved in mentoring programs for children and young adults. Charity work does not always involve money. Sometimes a person's time and commitment to a community can be just as rewarding. According to Mignon, "God has called me to be generous. He has commanded me to use my business as a resource to other people." Mignon strongly believes that if you give more to your community, then your community will give back more to you.

I asked Mignon where she sees her company going in the next five years, and she couldn't give me an answer, for a good reason. She could not have dreamed it was going to be as big as it is now and wants to follow whatever plan God has for her. Her belief is that God is in control of everything, and she is just as excited as everyone else to know what God has in store for her. Mignon believes that God has put wonderful people in her life, and He will reveal the next revelation for her plans when the time is right. As a final note, I asked Mignon what advice would she give to somebody starting a business. She left me with the following words:

> I would tell somebody to not be afraid and to move in courage, by knowing you can have anything that you want if you set your mind to it. We are only limited by the things we think we cannot do. The biggest thing is to start walking, because as you walk you will find that God is already saying 'Come on I'm waiting! Catch up to me.' As long as you are trying to walk in purpose, He created you for something. If you learn to seek out your purpose and your life's goal, everything is going to fall into place like it's supposed to.

After analyzing Mignon's powerful story, the first thing I noticed was that all of the keys of knowledge contributed to her success. The keys that she applied the most were creativity, discipline, God, faith, and courage. With Mignon's creativity, she was able to create a thriving business without incurring a large amount of debt. She stated several times that she needed to be creative since cash flow was a major problem for her. A lack of money keeps many people from going into business, but many people don't realize that creativity can reduce or even eliminate the need for money. A person should not let money be the determining factor of whether or not to start a business. Get creative and make your dreams come true.

For Mignon to be able to feed her entire family with $5, it definitely took a level of discipline that many people don't have. Remember, you have to sacrifice many things in the short term to get where you want to be in the long term. In Mignon's case a full-course meal was a major sacrifice for her family as well. I found it very extraordinary that she was able to get her entire family to be disciplined as well, when it came to money. Even though things were falling apart for her financially, Mignon kept her discipline and remained focused on the bigger picture. She had to have discipline in her budget, quality of life, and work ethic to ultimately get the things she wanted.

God was the key of knowledge that Mignon used the most. Her entire planning was based off her belief in God, and she didn't make one decision without praying about it first. Many people claim that they believe in God but fail to incorporate Him in their daily lives. Mignon believes that if you are ashamed of God, then He will be ashamed of you. Not only was she not ashamed, but Mignon was willing to tell anybody what God had done for her and her family. Once again, I do not want to persuade anyone's beliefs or how they view the world, but you just can't write off Mignon's success as a coincidence or chance. She believed that there was divine intervention in her actions, and it's hard to ignore her claim with the level of success she has had. Mignon went from poverty to prosperity in less than two years, and she credits all of her success to her belief in God.

Faith was a major key in Mignon's success. When everything around her seemed hopeless, she had faith in God and herself that The Cupcake Collection would be a reality. You have to have undying faith that your objectives can and will be achieved. What if Mignon lacked the faith to open her business, when the NES truck was around the corner or when the house was in foreclosure? She would probably be in the same situation she was in two years ago, struggling to survive. Even when Xavier had doubt that they could get the house they wanted, Mignon stuck to her faith and refused to take no for an answer. A person's faith doesn't get stronger when everything is going great. It gets stronger when everything around a person is falling apart, and he or she refuses to quit.

One of the first things Mignon said about God is that He doesn't like a wimp. Courage is the cornerstone of a successful business. It takes courage to start a business in the first place. Many people are too afraid to take the destiny out of an employer's hands and put it into their own hands. Owning a business is not for the weak at heart. Every adversity you can think of will come running your way the day you decide to become an entrepreneur. Mignon was not afraid of her adversities, and she didn't run from them either. She took on every adversity that came her way. Having courage does not mean that you lack fear, but it's the ability to put your fear behind you and have a brave front to overcome your challenges.

The two competitive advantages Mignon created in her business were being a low-cost leader in her industry and being able to differentiate her products and services. Being the low-cost leader in an industry doesn't always mean you have the lowest price for your products or services. It can also mean you are able to produce your products and services cheaper than competitors. Mignon was able to do this by being efficient in her operations. She was able to lower her operational costs by running her business out of her home and employing members of her family to run the bakery. All of her advertising has been word-of-mouth, which is absolutely free. This allowed her to purchase many items for her business without a loan. Mignon did not have the luxury of being able to go into the bank and get a big loan; she had to be creative and find other ways to start her business. This creativity enabled her to eliminate debt and keep overhead low. When it was time for her to purchase the cupcake bus, Mignon paid cash for it instead of taking out a loan. When Mignon decides to open up the bakery in Clarksville, the majority of the financing will come from her. Being the low-cost leader in an industry enables an organization to take advantage of many opportunities that competitors don't have.

The unique flavors and customer service that The Cupcake Collection offers cannot be easily duplicated or imitated. Mignon keeps the recipes for her cupcakes under lock and key, because her competitors would love to know what's in them. The first thing that many people ask when they bite into Mignon's cupcakes is, "what is in this?" All of her cupcakes are made from scratch, so you can't go to the grocery store and create the same cupcakes at home if you tried. Betty Crocker is not going to help you reproduce one of Mignon's cupcakes. You have to go into her bakery if you want the same quality and taste. Mignon's customer service is impeccable. The Cupcake Collection treats customers like family, and that is one of the main reasons they keep coming back. Establishing a personal relationship with customers can be a challenge, and Mignon has capitalized on this advantage. She offers a unique product with a unique service. Where else can you go and get a free cupcake when you are having a bad day? Mignon offers free cupcakes and advice to anyone who needs them. These are the types of products and services that you want to offer in order to create a competitive advantage.

The main lesson that I learned from Mignon's case study is to never give up on God, your dreams, or yourself. When you are trying to do something positive with your life, there will be many critics waiting on you to fail. The reason they want you to fail is that they don't have the courage to step out on faith and make their dreams come true. After reading Mignon's case study, there is no reason for you to lack courage. This woman was faced with adversities that would have destroyed a weak person. When you decide to be bold and courageous in your efforts to be successful, opportunities you never thought were possible will come your way.

PART THREE
THE WHITE COLLAR

7 THE ACTION PLAN FOR
CORPORATE HUSTLERS

Unfortunately, too many people in our society are either underemployed or unemployed. This has to change, and we must depend on ourselves to change our current situations. When you decide to go to war with your circumstances, I want you to be armed with every weapon essential for victory. Having key knowledge on how to corporate hustle will be part of your war chest. Many people don't have, or even know how to create, a traditional job resume. The action plan for corporate hustlers is similar to a job resume, but much more powerful. This plan has been passed down through the hands of many successful corporate hustlers, and it has been perfected by everyone who has touched it. Contrary to popular belief, you want to have an action plan for every position you are trying to fill in Corporate America. Even if you are applying for a hustle at McDonald's, you want to have an action plan tailored for the position. Why? The action plan automatically gives you a competitive advantage over your competition. At this point, you should know that any traditional job is viewed as an opportunity to make money, and the employer is a corporate customer who has given you an opportunity to corporate hustle. You are now a boss, and every action that you take is to improve your business and your situation. This includes accepting a position that you normally wouldn't take. If you still haven't let go of your pride, you will not benefit from this plan. If you have let it go, then it's time to make some money.

Remember, this is just a daytime hustle, and you are creating a grand plan by night or whenever you are not hustling. The first thing you must do before creating the action plan is to identify your enemies. Who are your enemies? They are the ones or entities holding you back from accomplishing your goal of acquiring a corporate customer. Your enemies can be hard to identify sometimes because they come in many forms. Many of

120

them hide behind excuses for not giving you an opportunity to make money. The excuses that an enemy will use are: you're overqualified; you don't have the experience; you don't have the education; you have a criminal record; we are not hiring; or whatever the excuses may be. If you have ever heard any of these excuses, then it should not be as hard now to identify your enemies. In other situations the enemy could be you. If you are not equipped with the tools in your war chest that will give you a competitive advantage in Corporate America, then you are your own worst enemy. Competitive advantages in the workplace are:

1. Higher education
2. Higher levels of certifications and training
3. Professional appearance
4. Good hygiene
5. Excellent code switcher
6. Reliable transportation
7. Valid form of I.D.

Even though most of these competitive advantages should be self-explanatory, many people are either unaware or missing key components on this list. As discussed earlier, I believe a high-school education or a GED is essential for getting most corporate positions. Along with a basic education, many corporations require individuals to have advanced education as well. If you believe college is not for you, the next best thing is to attend a community college and take at least one class. Yes! I said one class. One class is the difference between you listing "some college" or "high-school graduate" on an employment application. You have to try your best to eliminate every excuse a corporation can use to discriminate against you.

It doesn't matter what subject your one class is. The main thing is to choose a subject you enjoy, and you do well in the course. One of best classes to take is English 100 or 101. This one class will help you become a better writer and communicator in the long term. These are the attributes a company desires in a corporate hustler. If you are absolutely sure that you are not going to college, then you should take a serious look at getting training or a certification in a desired trait. Recall Mark's case. When he was released from prison, he had to get certified as a general contractor before he could start making millions of dollars. If you can't afford to go to school or get the proper training, look at the federal government for assistance. The government either gives or loans millions of dollars in financial aid a year. This money is for the disenfranchised, and more Americans should capitalize on this opportunity. If you don't, someone else definitely will. At all costs, try to avoid student loans. A grant is the better option because it does not have to be paid back. If you do have to get a student loan, borrow only what you can afford to "repay."

Ever since I was in the 7th grade, I've been wearing Ralph Lauren Polo shirts as part of my personal style. I'm not trying to brag about my expensive taste in clothing, only prove a valid point. You don't have to be wealthy or have a substantial amount of money to have nice cloths. The interesting fact about my Polo shirts is that my parents and sister used to buy them at the Goodwill store. There is no excuse for not being professionally dressed in the business environment. The Goodwill and other thrift stores are excellent places to purchase the business attire you need for Corporate America. You need to have a professional appearance in Corporate America to create a competitive advantage. Over 20 years ago, my late grandfather, Edgar, told me that "every man should own two black suits, two white shirts, five dark-colored ties, and two pairs of black-dress shoes." This statement holds true today. Women should have these same items, except for the ties of course. Granddaddy was trying to tell me, in his subtle and intelligent way, that a person has to dress for success. You could purchase all of the items I just listed for less than $40 at a thrift store. One thing many people don't know about most thrift stores is that they clean their items before putting them on the racks.

Remember, this book is not for the "haves" but for the "have nots." I'm thinking of the individuals who have nothing and want to change their lives. Money will be an issue for many of these individuals, and they need to know how to get on their feet quickly and be prepared for battle. There are unwritten rules in Corporate America, and being professionally dressed is one of them. When you go for an interview with a potential corporate customer, they expect you to know these rules. A person never wants to go on an interview with anything or wearing anything that will distract the interviewer. This includes loud colors, highly fashionable clothing, or a significant amount of jewelry, poor hygiene, or other major distractions. A clean white shirt, dark suit, and dark tie is the official battle-dress uniform (BDU) for Corporate America. The BDU must be subtle, signifying that you are ready for battle and can adapt to any situation. In the Army, my BDU was subdued with camouflage. You want to blend into the corporate environment and not stand out. Your performance will do that for you. The suit you wear should never have more than three buttons and should always be single breasted. Ladies, you could highlight certain assets of your figures that might give you the advantage for an interview with a man, but what if you were being interviewed by a woman? She could find your attire offensive. Always wear a dress or skirt that is no more than one inch above your knee; and excessive cleavage should always be avoided as well. You don't know who your opponent in battle will be, so be prepared for any situation.

You would be surprised how many people I have interviewed in my career with poor hygiene. People would want me to hire them, and I just wanted them to get out of my presence with that bad breath or terrible body odor! A person's personal appearance and hygiene speak volumes about his or her work performance. If a person doesn't take the time to take care of themselves, why would a corporate customer think that individual would take care of their company? If you don't have access to clean water, you can simply go to a gas station and take a bird bath. I believe a bird bath is self-explanatory in this situation. Always take a bath or shower the day of the interview.

Do not use cologne or perfume. The best thing to do is use soap with a good, strong fragrance to highlight your cleanliness; deodorant is mandatory as well. Men, make sure you have a fresh haircut and shave. Ladies, make sure your hair is presentable and not looking like you just got out of bed. These are actual circumstances I have experienced when I interviewed individuals for employment. Poor hygiene will get you disqualified for a corporate position very quickly.

Code switching takes place in Corporate America everyday. This is a term used in anthropology to describe an individual's ability to switch his or her language dialog. An example of this would be the difference in a conversation you would have with friends compared to one with a corporate customer. If you are talking to your friends, there is nothing wrong with calling them dude, big head, pal, or whatever terms you use to express endearment. This type of dialog will not get you into Corporate America. When you are interviewing with a corporate customer, always show a high level of respect and courtesy. You should address your interviewer as "sir" or "ma'am," and you should respond to questions with "sir" or "ma'am" as well. If your interviewer asks you, "do you believe you are qualified for this position," you should respond to him with "yes sir, I believe I am highly qualified for this position." If your interviewer asks you, "have you ever performed this type of work," you should respond to her, "yes ma'am, I have over two years of experience." I think you get the point. Even though you might not be an eloquent speaker, or very articulate, having good manners will take you a long way.

One of the greatest tools that a corporate hustler can have is reliable transportation. Many people lose incredible opportunities with corporate customers because they missed or were late to an important interview, due to a lack of transportation. When you are late to an interview, the interviewer will often tell you that the interview is already over before you even begin. Being on time for an interview is serious business. I recommend you get to an interview at least 30 minutes early. This shows the corporate customer you are serious about the opportunity, and being on time is one of your key attributes. If you don't have reliable transportation, make sure you take advantage of the public transportation in your area. Know that bus or train schedule like the back of your hand.

In a "Post 911" society, a valid form of I.D. is a must. The best form of I.D. is a state-issued driver's license. A valid driver's license shows that you are responsible and more than likely have transportation. Even if you don't have a car, you should definitely try to obtain a driver's license. Another excellent form of I.D. is a passport. I recommend that everyone, who is able, obtain a passport. A passport signifies that a person is well-rounded and willing to travel if required. If you can't obtain a driver's license or a passport, the next best thing is a valid state I.D. Everyone must have a valid social-security number to work in the United States. Sometimes, a social-security card can take a while to obtain. If you don't have one, you should order one as soon as possible.

Creating the Action Plan

After you have identified your competitive advantages, you want to gather as much information as you can for the purpose of creating a sound action plan. An information sheet is the best way to get started, so you will have everything you need before you start writing the plan. An information sheet should consist of the following information:

1. Former corporate customers (employers) with their addresses and phone numbers
2. Names of relatives with their addresses and phone numbers
3. Names of references with their addresses and phone numbers
4. Schools and training courses attended

Other information that should be listed on this sheet includes your former job positions with the dates you held the positions.

Once you have gathered all the required information, you should begin to create your action plan (also known as a job resume). The action plan is simple to create, and it can be created on any word processor. If you don't have a computer, you can even use a typewriter to create it. The best thing to do if you don't have a computer or know how to type is to get someone else to create it for you. Write a legible action plan on paper and give it to the person who will create it for you. The basic format for the plan is a one-page document with one-inch margins. Your action plan should always be created on white, professional paper. It is extremely important to follow this format. I have used this format for several years, and it is highly effective. There is an example action plan on the following page.

John Smith

1234 Main St • Nashville, TN 37206 • (615) 555-1234 • johnsmith@email.com

---

Professional Summary

• Over six years of experience leading and working with diverse groups of individuals with
varied backgrounds, cultures, and nationalities
• Highly proficient in the use and operation of various computer systems, software,
databases and programs including: MS Word, Excel, PowerPoint, Access, and Outlook
• Exceptional interpersonal and communications skills with the ability to establish quality
rapport with customers, subordinates, peers, and upper management
• Excellent clerical skills which include being able to type 50 words per minute and
maintaining filing systems and office records/files

Education
Associate of Arts in General Studies, Nashville State Community College, Nashville, TN 37209
(2007-2009)

Professional Training
Human Resources Certification, United States Army, Fort Knox, KY 40121 (2000-2001)

Professional Experience and Achievements
Office Task Force Employment Agency, Nashville, TN 37205 (2009-Present)
Position: Office Automations Technician
• Responsible for reviewing and processing incoming and outgoing correspondence
• Assisted in interviewing individuals, collecting, obtaining and analyzing information,
examining records, and preparing personnel reports
• Performed administrative functions which included communicating work assignments, in
writing, with hiring parties

Freight Express, Inc., Nashville, TN 37207 (2005-2009)
Position: Dispatch Technician
• Responsible for the dispatching, planning, management, and safety of over 200 road
drivers and movement of less-than-truckload freight
• Conducted safety briefings, evaluations, and inspections in accordance with U.S.
Department of Transportation
• Performed clerical/administrative functions which included creating reports using MS
Office applications and AS400 mainframe, and filing driver records/files

Figure 2

I have talked and worked with several human resources (HR) recruiters, and most of them told me that they will throw a resume in the garbage if it's longer than one page and not white. HR recruiters have to look through hundreds, sometimes thousands, of resumes at a time. They will find any reason to toss your action plan in the trash. The last thing they want to do is read through a two or three-page document. The font size should be set on 12, and check the plan several times for misspelled words. An action plan should be short, precise, and identify the key attributes that make you eligible for a position. The following sections should be in your plan:

1. Contact information

2. Professional summary

3. Education

4. Professional Training

5. Professional experience and achievements

Refer to the example action plan in figure 2 for suggested formatting, bulleting and bordering. Your contact information should begin with your name centered at the top. The second line is also centered with your address, contact phone number, and email address. Both lines should be typed in bold print. Never list your social-security number in the plan. You can give that information later if the corporation is serious about hiring you. The title of each section, borders, and bullets are in bold text as well. The professional summary should begin with how much experience you have, and you should never list over 10 years of experience. Some corporations will view candidates with too much experience as hard to train and not willing to learn a new system. Complete sentences are not used in the plan. Each phrase begins with a strong action word. In the professional summary, begin each phrase with a strong adjective that highlights your ability to exceed expectations, such as exceptional, excellent, or outstanding. This is your one shot at grabbing the attention of a recruiter, and action words will help keep their attention.

You should try your best not to make any phrases longer than two lines. Any phrases longer than two lines will also slow down the reader of your plan. Most of the time, when you read an advertisement for employment, there are qualifications for the position listed in the advertisement. These are normally referred to as "key words." The professional summary is the section in your plan where you want to list your key words. In the example plan, John is applying for a clerical position that requires him to type at least 40 words per minute. John was able to include the fact he can type 50 words per minute, exceeding the requirement. If an HR recruiter doesn't identify your qualifications right away, then the plan goes in the trash. Many corporations require you to submit your plan electronically. Recall, this was the position in which I found myself. I didn't get my federal position until a computer system recognized the key words in my action plan. If HR recruiters weren't bad enough, your plan could end up being thrown away by a computer. Identifying and listing key words in your plan is crucial.

The third section of the plan describes your level of education. Only list your highest level of completion. Many people have two and four-year degrees. Only list the four-year degree. If you have attended college but didn't graduate, you can simply list the school, major studied, and years of attendance. This still shows you have studied at a higher level of learning. The forth section of the plan will list your professional training. Any relevant professional training such as welding, plumbing, or computer certifications should be listed in the same format as education. Some individuals might not have professional training, but that won't hinder you in many situations. If you do have professional training, it should be listed under education with its own title.

The last section of the plan describes your professional experience and achievements. This is the section where you justify why you are qualified to fill the position that you're seeking. Once again, you want to make sure the key words that the position requires are in this section as well. I also want you to notice the strong action words that begin each phrase in the example plan. Words such as assisted, conducted, responsible, performed, and supervised reflect your ability to take responsibility of any tasks given to you. Many people make the mistake of listing awards, recognitions, and other achievements that do not necessarily reflect your experience. Every phrase in this section should be work related and highlight the level of responsibility you have had in the past. For anyone that has military experience, you should try your best to make your military experience reflect your ability to carry out the same type of work, in a civilian setting. Employers will sometimes view your military experience as irrelevant, unless you are able to show that the duties can be conducted in a normal work environment.

The Search

After you have completed your basic action plan, you want to begin your search for a corporate position. This will often be your biggest challenge, because many corporations are seeking corporate hustlers with specific qualifications, and you have to tailor your action plan to match each corporate position. Some of the most common resources that people use to find a corporate position are:

1. Newspapers

2. Online job banks

3. Job fairs

4. Employment agencies/temporary services

5. Scanning the environment for "help wanted" signs

FROM NO COLLAR TO A WHITE COLLAR

6. Company websites

7. Unemployment offices

If you have not exhausted every resource on the above list for a corporate position, then you have room to improve your search for a corporate hustle. Companies still advertise employment opportunities in local newspapers, and the Sunday paper usually has the most opportunities for employment. If you do find an employment opportunity in the newspaper, respond to it immediately. You are not the only one scanning the newspaper for employment. Job banks such as Monster and Career Builder are good resources for online employment searches. Many of these sites require you to upload your action plan and fill in other employment-related information. The task can seem tedious, but you just have to be patient and get through the process. When it comes to job fairs, they are one of the best places to find a corporate hustle. The companies at job fairs need people immediately, and many of them will hire you right on the spot. Anytime you go to a job fair, make sure you have at least 20 copies of your action plan with you. You definitely want to dress for success at a job fair by wearing your corporate BDU.

Another excellent place for finding corporate hustles is an employment agency or temporary service. People will often overlook opportunities from employment agencies due to the fact many of their positions are temporary. What many people fail to realize is that many temporary positions turn into full-time employment. You have to stay focused on your hustle and be willing to accept any opportunity that comes your way. The traditional way to look for a corporate hustle is scanning the environment for "help wanted" signs. Some companies choose not to advertise their employment opportunities online or in a newspaper. Always be on the lookout for "help wanted" signs, and you will have a good chance of finding a company willing to give you an opportunity.

JOBS AVAILABLE

✳ **Above Average Income**

✳ **3 To 5 Hour Average Shifts**

✳ **Will Work Around Your Schedule**

APPLY INSIDE

Many companies also have their own websites for finding corporate hustlers. These positions are not advertised anywhere except the company website. Make sure you search for these opportunities as well. The last place people go to find a corporate hustle might be one of the best places to search. Many people will take advantage of unemployment insurance for the purpose of getting a weekly check, but the unemployment office receives a significant amount of referrals for employment as well. The most important thing to keep in mind is to never give up. The moment you decide to give up is when you are most likely to miss an opportunity to get money.

The Interview

After you have taken advantage of the many resources to find a corporate customer, you have a very good chance of receiving a response from one of them. As a precaution, make sure the phone number you listed in your contact information is set up for a business call. In other words, you should not have a ring-back tone when a potential corporate customer calls your phone. Companies will simply hang up and dial the next person. Ring-back tones give the impression that you are not professional and lack maturity. When you are given the opportunity to interview with a corporate customer, the first thing you want to do is get as much information on the company as possible. At the very least, know the company's mission and vision statements. You should also know the basic duties and functions of the position you are being considered to fill.

This shows the company you have enough initiative to research the position, giving you a competitive advantage over other candidates. Not only do you want to dress for success, but you want to overdress for the interview as well. If you are going to interview for a position at McDonald's, you want to show up wearing a white shirt, black slacks, and black dress shoes. The other candidates will probably show up wearing casual clothing. This again shows how serious you are about getting the position. If an interview only requires you to wear a shirt and tie, you want to show up wearing a suit and tie for the purpose of out shining the other candidates. The items you should take with you to an interview are: five copies of your action plan, your information sheet, picture ID, social-security card, and a good pen. Corporate customers will often have additional paperwork for you to fill out, along with submitting your action plan. A significant amount of this additional information will be located on your information sheet. Another important issue is being organized. You should not show up to an interview shuffling paperwork. Have all of your paperwork in a small, black binder. This will give you the professionalism corporate customers seek.

When it comes to the actual interview, maintain good eye contact at all times. If you look down at the floor and not directly into the eyes of the interviewer, it gives them the impression that you are not confident in yourself and intimidated by the interview. Never let an interviewer intimidate you. You should have a high level of confidence, but make sure your confidence is not interpreted as arrogance. Begin the interview with a handshake and thank the interviewer for taking the time to meet with you. Always keep your hands in your lap during the entire interview. If you have a tendency to talk with your hands, this can be distracting to the interviewer. If, at anytime during the interview, you are asked a question you can't answer, tell the interviewer that you will research the answer and give it to them at a later time. An interviewer will know very quickly if you're simply making things up, just for the sake of giving an answer.

At the end of the interview, make sure you shake the person's hand and thank them for the interview a second time. You should also get the person's contact information, so you can send them a thank you correspondence for the interview and communicate that you are looking forward to hearing back from the company. Many people think the interview process is the last impression they will leave with the corporate customer. A follow-up correspondence will always give you an edge on other candidates, because so many people simply don't do it. Finding corporate customers in a recession can be a daunting task, but now you have the tools and knowledge that will make you stand out in an oversaturated market of corporate hustlers. If you are able to capitalize on all of the competitive advantages of a corporate hustler, you will definitely be ahead of the game. I believe Denzel Washington said it best in the movie "Training Day." Denzel's character, Alonzo, stated that the game is chess and not checkers![12] Each move you make should to be a calculated one. This will allow you to beat your opponent at their own game.

Independent Hustling = Dedication
(The back of my photographer's car)

8 THE ACTION PLAN FOR INDEPENDENT HUSTLERS

Before I became an independent hustler, I was a slave. The slavery I am referring to is economic slavery. My chains of bondage were overwhelming debt and my dependence on a corporate position. Now, I am economically and financially prepared for any situation that tries to take my economic freedom. Unlike physical slavery, economic slavery doesn't target a particular ethnic group or discriminate against a particular gender. It only knows one color, and that color is green. The only thing economic slavery wants is your money and the freedom that comes with it. I believe in having a corporate hustle, but there will come a time when your autonomy is more important than a comfort zone. When you really think about it, there is absolutely nothing comfortable about an entity having the power over you to say, "you're fired," and your entire life gets turned upside down. When a bank can come and tell you, "this is our house now," that is not a comfortable feeling. When a finance company can knock on your door and tell you, "we need the keys to your car," how is that really a comfort zone? If you believe "slave" is a strong term for being economically disenfranchised, examine the definition of a slave. According to the dictionary, a slave is a "person who is the legal property and has to serve another...helpless victim of some dominating influence...workhorse, hack, laborer."[13] Does that description sound familiar to you?

When an individual lives from paycheck-to-paycheck, it creates a helpless, weak, and hopeless feeling. Don't be a slave to your debt or economic situation. Use your mind to gain independence from the tyranny of bondage. Freedom over your situation must manifest from thought before it can become reality. You have to create options for yourself, and that is what independent hustling enables an individual to do. Do I believe the system is designed for individuals to fail? Yes, the system is designed for certain individuals to fail. If you are weak, ignorant, and afraid to get out of your comfort zone, then the system is designed for you to fail. What is the system? The system is "capitalism." The types of individuals who fail in a capitalistic society are the ones who are reactive instead of proactive. Capitalism destroys weak individuals and rewards individuals who are not afraid to step out on faith. According to the Scripture, "for God hath not given us the spirit of fear; but of power, and love, and of a sound mind" (II Timothy, 1:7, KJV). It's time for individuals to stop fearing the system, tap into their power, love themselves, and use the sound minds God gave them.

An independent hustler refuses to be weak and always prepares for war. There are always wars to be fought in a capitalistic society. If you are not battling fuel costs one minute, you are battling to keep your job the next. When you finally have enough money to put gas in your car, you hear about a big layoff coming at work. Once you have survived the latest layoff, your electricity gets disconnected. Be prepared for the ceiling to cave in on your head at anytime. If a corporate customer terminates your services, have a small business in place that was demanding more of your attention anyway. Having this type of flexibility gives you the ability to be prepared for any economic war you will fight. An independent hustler can adapt to any economic condition.

When the U.S economy really began to get worse in 2008, individuals on Wall Street, who were accustomed to making six and seven-figure incomes, were finding themselves financially ruined and unemployed. Economic slavery has sympathy for no one. An independent hustle is essential for a multi-hustler to create a six-figure income. Many individuals don't have a choice but to become an independent hustler. No matter how members of our society claim that ex-convicts are given a second chance, there are individuals who will never be given an opportunity to corporate hustle because of a criminal past. To overcome this, many ex-convicts return to a life of crime, and they end up back in the penitentiary. This is absolutely the wrong approach, and that is what the system wants individuals to do. Make no mistake about it, capitalism benefits from crime in the 21st century. The reason it does is that many prisons are now owned by private institutions. A private institution is just another way of describing a profit-generating entity. If you have been denied a corporate hustle due to a criminal record, remember Mark's story. He didn't become a millionaire from corporate hustling. His millions came from independent hustling in the construction industry. A million-dollar hustle is not reality right now, but generating a six-figure income would be an excellent start. Creating an independent hustle involves the following three actions:

1. Legalizing the dream
2. Writing the dream
3. Financing the dream

Legalizing the Dream

When you decide to legalize the dream, you have to choose the right business structure and file the proper documents for your business to be a legal entity. There are many types of business, but I will only focus on three types. Sole proprietorships, partnerships, and limited-liability companies (LLC) are the three types of business best suited for an independent hustle. The most common business structure is a sole proprietorship. As the name suggests, this type of organization is operated by one person. One of the biggest advantages of a sole proprietorship is complete autonomy. You are the boss, and no one has control over any decision you make. Even your income taxes for the business can be included in your personal income taxes. This alleviates many of the tax issues associated with other business structures. Another advantage of a sole proprietorship is limited government interference. The last thing you want is a significant amount of government interference when you are trying to operate a business. One of the biggest disadvantages of a sole proprietorship is unlimited liability.

Unlimited liability means that you are solely responsible for any debt or financial obligations associated with the business. If you default on a loan, or the business gets sued, the bank or suing party can go after any personal assets that belong to you. This means that you could lose your house, car, and other properties associated with your personal assets. Many people are willing to accept unlimited liability, as long as they can have full autonomy over their business.

The next business structure commonly associated with entrepreneurship is a partnership. A partnership is almost identical to a sole proprietorship, but it's owned and operated by two or more individuals. It is up to the partners whether they will share the same percentage in the business, or each partner will have different levels of responsibility. To ensure that every member of the organization is in full cooperation, a formal agreement should be created to address major issues such as responsibilities, ownership, and termination of ownership. If one of the partners die, their percentage of the business doesn't necessarily go to the remaining partners. That is why it is so important to have a contract in place before unforeseen events occur. As with a sole proprietorship, the partners have unlimited liability and take on the risk of losing their personal assets. Many people simply like the freedom that sole proprietorships and partnerships allow them to have. These types of business structures are simple to initiate and don't involve a significant amount of paperwork.

Unlike the first two business structures, an LLC is considered a completely separate entity from the actual owners. I personally think that this is the best business structure for a small business. What is the use of making a six-figure income when someone can take it all away from you with a frivolous lawsuit? An LLC protects you from most liabilities that can occur from owning a business. As far as taxes are concerned, you do have to file separate taxes on behalf of your company. To establish my organization as an LLC, the only thing I did was go down to the Secretary of State's office for Tennessee and filed the proper documents. I had to pay an initial fee of $300 and a filing fee of $20. These prices differ from state to state, so make sure you do the proper research before you plan to establish an LLC. I also had to pay an annual fee of $300 for having an LLC, and the money was well worth it. If my company went into debt, the debtors would have to go after the LLC and not my personal assets. An annual fee of $300 is a small price to pay for a peace of mind.

Once you have decided on what type of business structure you want for your organization, then your next step should be filing the proper documents. For most businesses, you will need to register your business name, obtain a business license, and apply for an employer identification number (EIN). Before you can use the name you have created for your business, you want to make sure it is not already in existence. To do this, you should go to the secretary of state's office for your particular state, and the office can check the availability of your business name. This will ensure that you don't end up in a legal battle over the name of your company. You can also register trademarks in the same location. Registering your business name also prevents others from using your name.

A business license gives you the right to sell your goods or services in the state where you are operating. To obtain a business license, you must go to your county clerk's office or the tax division for your state. The license also requires you to track and pay sales taxes for your state. If you are caught operating a business without a business license, it could result in hefty fines or the loss of your business. Even though you may not have a physical location for your business because you only sell products/services online, you still want to acquire a business license from the state where you reside. If you conduct business outside of the state where you operate, you may still be required to obtain a business license from each state where you conduct business. An EIN is the same as a federal tax identification number, and it is required for the purpose of filing federal income taxes for your business. You can request this number from the IRS Website at http://www.irs.gov.[14] Having an EIN also gives you access to companies that only deal with legitimate businesses. For example, my friend Judah buys several goods from wholesalers and sells the goods at retail prices. Without an EIN, many of these companies would not allow him to purchase items in bulk. Many wholesalers do not sell goods to the general public. Having your organization properly registered and documented will open up many doors that would otherwise be closed to you.

A registered business name, business license, and EIN are essential for you to have a legitimate business; but there may be additional industry-related requirements for you to operate. To become a general contractor, Mark had to obtain a general contractor's license. He also has to obtain the required permits from the code's office to operate on his construction sites. For Mignon to operate her bakery, she has to meet the food and safety requirements established by the local health department. If Mignon fails an inspection given by the health department, her bakery could get shut down. Do your research to make sure you are in compliance with any rules and regulations that govern your industry. Independent hustlers can lose a significant amount of time and money if their businesses are not operating legitimately. A good online resource for finding industry requirements for operating a particular business is http://www.business.gov.[15] The information available on the Website is from several government sources, and it will save you a significant amount of time compared to searching for the same information on your own. If you plan on hiring employees, you will have to file additional documents and be in compliance with the U.S. Department of Labor (DOL). Visit the DOL office for your state to obtain the information related to having employees. Many states have their own DOL Website you can access for information as well.

Writing the Dream

Once you have legalized the dream, then it will be time to write it in the form of a business plan. A business plan is the blueprint for how your organization will conduct operations, make a profit, finance the business, and who will be involved in the business. If you are planning on having investors or obtaining financing for your company, you will definitely need a business plan. Creating a business plan is not as difficult as you think. Many independent hustlers choose to hire someone to create a business plan for them. If you have the time, knowledge, and patience to create a business plan on your own, you can save yourself a significant amount of money. Business consultants will charge you hundreds, if not thousands, of dollars to create a business plan for your organization. I suggest you get on a serious hustle and create a business plan on your own. There are several sources for obtaining information on creating a business plan. I have seen computer software for creating business plans cost as much as $600. Don't go out and spend that type of money to create a business plan, instead go to the Small Business Administration (SBA) Website at http://www.sba.gov and create your business plan for free.[16] As I mentioned earlier, the SBA is a great source for finding funding for small businesses; it also offers a substantial amount of information on helping individuals start a business, including templates for business plans.

A business plan is not the same as the grand plan you created for your business, but you should be able to use a significant amount of information from it to create your business plan. According to the SBA, a sound business plan should contain the following information:

1. Introduction

- Give a detailed description of the business and its goals

- Discuss ownership of the business and its legal structure

2. Marketing

• Discuss the products and services your company will offer

• Identify customer demand for your products and services

3. Financial Management

• Develop an expected return on investment and monthly cash flows for the first year

• Provide projected income statements and balance sheets for the for a two-year period

4. Operations

• Explain how the business will be managed day-to-day

• Discuss hiring and personnel procedures

5. Conclusion statement

• Summarize your business goals and objectives and express your

commitment to the success of your business[16]

This is just a glimpse of the information that needs to go into a business plan. Again, go to the SBA Website for additional information that will help you create a business plan and much more. I find it amazing that more people do not take advantage of the services offered by the SBA. Make sure you are not one of the lost souls out there claiming they can't see the forest because of all of the trees. Open your eyes and become aware of your surroundings. That is the only way you are going to succeed as an independent hustler. In today's society, an individual's attention span is short. Make your business plan short and to the point. I wouldn't recommend a business plan over 7-10 pages for a small business. You might even be able to create one that is only 4-6 pages. The key is capturing the reader's attention in the introduction or executive summary. That is the best place to sell your ideas in the business plan.

Financing the Dream

The last item that's needed to make your dreams a reality is financing. There are several sources you can tap into for the purpose of starting your business. When I conducted my research on this subject, I was surprised how much free money is available for entrepreneurs. I found the following sources that will help you finance your dream:

1. Private investors
2. Patrons
3. Peer-to-peer lending
4. Grants
5. Bank loans
6. Home equity/lines of credit
7. Title loans

I believe it's essential to have a sound business plan in place to present to any potential investor. This holds true for private investors as well. If you ever try to obtain financing from private investors, such as friends, family, and other key associates, they want to know that you are serious about your success. Your success means that they will get a return on their investments. I suggest that you ask private investors for financing in a professional manner. Have a formal presentation highlighting the core aspects of your business plan. Make sure you provide them with a copy of your business plan and have them sign a nondisclosure agreement, so your plan doesn't end up in the wrong hands.

Before I get into patron financing, I want to examine the word patron. According to the dictionary, a patron is "a wealthy or influential supporter of an artist or writer...one that uses wealth or influence to help an individual, an institution, or a cause."[17] I was absolutely blown away when I discovered that

144

there are wealthy individuals who help small businesses, by providing them with start-up money. Do you find this hard to believe? Well, let me validate this argument for you. One of my favorite reporters on CNN, Christine Romans, recently did a story on alternative ways to fund a small business.[18] Being the independent hustler that I am, I perked right up when I heard her discussing ways to get money. The basis of her story was patron financing. There are organizations who will help you find patrons for your business, and the patrons will give you hundreds, if not thousands, of dollars to help you start your company. In return, some organizations that helped you find the funding may require you to offer them ownership in your company. The percentage of ownership depends on the organization. A few organizations require you to give them as much as 30% ownership, and some ask for a small percentage such as 6% ownership. Some of these companies simply require you to give patrons discounts on your products or services.

The organization that really fascinated me was Kickstarter.com. The company has only been in existence since 2009. It has already had 200,000 patrons, worldwide, donate over $20,000,000 to entrepreneurs.[19] The process for getting this money is very simple. You send Kickstarter.com your business plan or idea. If your independent hustle is approved, then the company sets up a page for you with a fundraising goal. Backers of your plan donate cash, and they receive rewards from Kickstarter.com for their patronage. When I visited the Website, independent hustlers were getting anywhere from $400 to $900,000 for their plans! This was absolutely incredible. Even though Kickstarter.com is an outstanding source for patron financing, it is not the only one in existence.

Another company that I found offering patron financing was Techstars.org. The company's operations were similar to Kickstarter.com, but Techstars.org has a limit on how much you can raise. You are only allowed to receive up to $18,000, and the company requires a 6% stake in your company.[20] According to your hustle, 6% could be a lot or a little. It all depends on your ultimate goal for success. For a company to give me $18,000 without a loan, 6% ownership of my organization might not be a bad agreement. The third company that I found was Ycombinator.com. Compared to the other patron financers, this company has more restrictions for receiving funding. Ycombinator.com only distributes funding twice a year and offers up to $18,000 to start a business.[21] The company also requires you to spend three months in California for an intense training course. The training course consists of classes taught by successful independent hustlers who give you the ends and outs of entrepreneurship. They also have specialists for your specific industry. If you have the time and are selected for the program, the three months you spend in California will be well worth the funding and advice you will receive. Before you decide to apply for funding from a patron financer, do the necessary research to make sure it is for you.

Another opportunity for you to receive free money for your small business is through grants. A grant is very similar to patron financing, except you do not have to give up ownership in your company to receive the free money. A significant number of grants are given out by public and private institutions for the purpose of stimulating growth through small businesses. Many companies give away millions of dollars in grants a year, but many people do not take advantage of this opportunity. Many people do not know about the grants or have the knowledge on how to apply for them. The best place to go and find out about these grants is, once again, the SBA. The SBA has access to these grants and can help you create a grant proposal for receiving funding. The money is out there, but you have to be willing to put in the effort to go get it.

The last four sources of financing require you to pay back any funding you receive, with interest. The first recommended source is a peer-to-peer lender (PPL). Receiving funds from a PPL is not the same as applying for a conventional bank loan. The borrowers are ordinary citizens looking for a nice return on their investments. The first PPL that I discovered was Prosper.com. According to Prosper.com:

• Borrowers with good credit (640+) post a loan listing and lenders invest $25 or more toward your loan

• The interest rate is fixed for the life of the loan and never changes

• Monthly payments are fixed and will be automatically deducted from your bank account

• There are no hidden fees and you can pay off the loan early with no penalty

• Prosper loans are unsecured, fixed rate personal loans with multiple terms[22]

The two items that really grabbed my attention were the required credit score and the use of unsecured loans. If you tried to receive a loan from a conventional bank, it will probably require you to have a credit score of 700 or higher. This is why I stressed the fact you have to get your credit in good standing. A poor credit score will hinder you from receiving a loan, even from a PPL. Since the loan is unsecured, you will not have to provide any collateral to receive funding. This means that you won't lose your house or car if you default on the loan. Other PPL's that I found were Virginmoney.com and Lendingtree.com. All of these companies have different terms for borrowing money, so you should research and compare different PPL's before you decide to apply for a loan.

A conventional bank loan is one of the most difficult forms of financing to receive, especially in a recession. Banks make sure that they will receive a return on their investments, if not, you will not receive one dime from them. Again, go to the SBA for help applying for a conventional bank loan. With the SBA's assistance you will gain access to bank funding that you didn't know existed. These loans will normally have better interests rates, compared to you getting a bank loan on your own. Another type of funding that you can receive from a bank is a home equity loan or line of credit. For example, let's say you own a house worth $200,000. You only owe $100,000 on your house. This means you have $100,000 in equity in your home. With this type of equity, you can go into a bank and borrow against that equity. In other words banks will allow you to open up a line of credit and use your home as collateral. With falling housing prices, high foreclosure rates, and weak banks, financial institutions are not as willing as they once were to offer home equity loans. Unless it is absolutely necessary, try to avoid using the equity in your home to get a loan. When I was laid off, I had no choice but to tap into my home equity. The last thing you want is to lose your home by using it as collateral. I know I keep stressing it, but don't try to get a loan or grant on your own without first seeking assistance from the SBA. The organization was created by the federal government, for you. Make sure you take full advantage of this opportunity.

The last form of financing is my least favorite. If you have exhausted every attempt you can think of to receive funding, you might be able to take out a title loan on your vehicle. This only works if your vehicle is paid in full. If you have paid off your car, you can go into a title loan company, such as TitleMax, and the company will lend you money for the title of your car.[23] Once you have paid the loan back, the company will then return your title. The only issue I have with these types of companies is the interest rates that they give borrowers. I have seen title loan companies requiring you to pay back almost 30% interest on top of the principle of the loan. They are also quick to repossess your car. If you are as much as one day late paying on the loan, they will come and repossess your vehicle. It's a win-win situation for the title loan companies. The majority of them offer you a loan much less than what the car is actually worth. When they do repossess your car and resell it, they are more than likely to make a profit from your misfortune. If you choose to take out a title loan, make sure you can afford the monthly payments and always search for the best interest rate.

After examining all of the information related to independent hustling, I hope you are beginning to feel the chains of economic slavery loosening. When I began independent hustling, I made many mistakes that caused me to lose a significant amount of money. After reading this chapter, you should be a little more educated than I was and make money instead of losing it. Take your time, gather sound information related to your business, and make smart decisions. I didn't know about patron financing when I started independent hustling. Now, you can get free money, and the only thing you have to do is offer some of your corporate stock to these companies. If you did have doubt about starting your own company, this chapter should have alleviated a large portion of that doubt. Don't be afraid of failure, because the rewards of success far outweigh any setbacks that you might have as an independent hustler.

NOTES:

Mark and Kim Musgrove

9 HOLDING ON TO WEALTH

One of the key factors that will hinder individuals from sustaining a six-figure income is the inability to manage money. When I was a full-time corporate hustler, I had a serious problem with holding on to the money I had made. The only thing I had was a checking account with direct deposit. Even though direct deposit is great for getting your money fast, it will make you spend it quickly as well. Once I became an independent hustler, I realized that my cash flow was not continuous. This actually helped me budget and save money better. I didn't become financially enlightened all on my own. To help me become more financially responsible, I enlisted the help of my good friend, Kim, of Musgrove Construction.

I believe there is a cliché that states, "behind every great man is a great woman." This definitely holds true for my friend Mark, since he is married to Kim. Kim is the Chief Financial Officer (CFO) for Musgrove Construction, and she also handles operations for the company as well. She is so proficient at saving and investing money that I had to get her to reveal some of her secrets. Surprisingly, she was very generous with the information, which I identified as Kim's theory. Over a period of 15 years, I have studied and practiced several financial theories for holding on to wealth. The reason I chose to focus on Kim's theory is that it's simple, it worked for me, and she is a certified hustler. Kim is no stranger to money because her father was a famous bank robber in the 1960's and 1970's. Her father robbed over 50 banks in the Midwest and escaped from prison on several occasions. Kim even remembers her grandmother, aunt, and the family preacher being arrested by the FBI, for aiding and abetting a fugitive. She could remember her family always having a new car in the driveway, and she never went without anything she needed or wanted.

Kim's father's activities didn't have a negative effect on her, but quite the opposite. According to Kim, the main lesson her father's life of crime taught her was that "you can't depend on no one but yourself to make things happen. Sometimes you have to take what belongs to you." Now, she understood the money her father was taking wasn't his, but he had the hustle to get out there and get it. The only thing she did was reapply his actions into legal hustling, and she turned the negative influence of his lifestyle into a positive one. When Kim met Mark, she was already making six figures by running a pest-control company. This is where she developed the valuable tools of investing, accounting, and managing finances. Musgrove Construction has made several million dollars since she took over as CFO, and the company is still growing. Instead of giving you some financial theory that doesn't even apply to today's tough economic times, I decided to share one with you that I know works, and that anyone can apply. According to Kim's theory, "every investment an entrepreneur makes has to be calculated, conservative, and tangible." This alludes to the fact that an independent hustler's cash flow is uncertain and vulnerable to changes in the economy. Kim's theory addresses four activities that are essential for holding on to wealth:

1. Saving your wealth

2. Investing your wealth

3. Money in giving back

4. Risk management

Saving Your Wealth

One of the most difficult activities for individuals to do is save money. To accomplish this difficult task, you have to maintain serious discipline. The bottom line is that you have to pay yourself. It doesn't matter if its $5, make sure you put some of your net income into a savings account. Recall Glen's case study. He stated that an individual needs to have five figures in their checking and savings accounts at all times. You have to start somewhere, so take the time and open up a savings account. It's a simple way to hold on to wealth, but you have to practice discipline to get your account up to $10,000. Kim also practices this method. She and Mark used to invest a significant amount of money in the stock market, but the losses they sustained in 2008 and 2009 were just too much. They lost approximately 40% of their savings in the stock market. After the financial collapse on Wall Street, many individuals began to take their money out of stocks and placed it in savings accounts. Although a savings account doesn't draw much interest, your money is secured up to $250,000 by the Federal Deposit Insurance Commission (FDIC). In other words, you don't have to worry about losing your money due to someone else's mistakes. A savings account is very conservative, but it's one of the most secure places you can put your money.

Investing Your Wealth

Once you begin to see results from your multi-hustle and savings efforts, it's time to invest your hard-earned money into something serious and tangible. That is why I still invest my money in real estate. Real estate is definitely a risk, but it's a calculated risk. If you haven't heard, the real-estate market is not dead! Every time I read a newspaper or see a newscast that states it is, it makes me boil inside. People are still getting significant returns from investing in real estate, including Mark and Kim. While Mark is the salesman in the family, Kim is definitely the investor and has been very successful at it. Her goal is to focus on long-term flips, compared to short-term profits. The shortest period Kim has ever flipped a house was three weeks. The longest she has ever taken to flip a house was three years.

The first thing she does is find a house that's listed way under its market value. For example, the home she flipped in

154

three weeks was purchased for $60,000. The house was appraised at $80,000 before any remodeling work had begun. This means she went into the house with $20,000 in equity. After spending a week giving the house a cosmetic makeover with new paint and appliances, Kim was able to sell the house for $115,000 two weeks later. Minus operations and closing costs, she made approximately $50,000. I asked Kim how she determines which flips will be short term and which ones will be long term. She stated that "if we have a house on the market for longer than six months, then it's time to convert it into a rental property." Kim also offers a lease-purchase option to her renters. Even though she isn't able to sell the house right away, the mortgage is still being paid by the renters every month. Not only is the mortgage being paid, but the home's equity increases at the same time. This is a win-win situation, and Kim used this strategy for the house that took three years to flip. She purchased the house for $70,000 and invested approximately $20,000 in it for renovations. When the house was sold three years later, it sold for $190,000. Mark and Kim made approximately $90,000 in profits at closing. I don't know about you, but I'm willing to wait three years to make $90,000 off one investment.

How was this possible? The most I had ever made from flipping a house was $15,000. At that point, I wanted to know the exact steps to finding a diamond in the ruff and converting it into a fortune. According to Kim:

> The first thing you want to find is the right neighborhood where houses are selling. Then you want to find a cheap house that needs lots of improvements. After that, you want to build the home up and out to the neighborhood's standard and not over and above it. It's about keeping the price within means of the neighborhood and furnishing someone with a good-quality home. Simple improvements to a home, such as updated

lighting, cabinet colors, new appliances, and new windows for a modern look, can easily add $40,000 to the selling price. The main factor is to have the home slightly under priced compared to other homes in the neighborhood.

She also recommended that you always get a good inspection of the home, so you know exactly what issues need to be addressed. Kim warned that you should never buy a home with foundation problems. Foundation problems can cost thousands of dollars to repair, and you will end up losing money instead of making it. The way Kim finds the houses is by word-of-mouth, through realtors. Good realtors are in-tune to what homes are available before they even hit the market. The reason Mark and Kim are so adamant about real estate is that houses are tangible items. They feel comfortable about being able to drive by and see a physical investment. It gives them a sense of control compared to losing thousands of dollars in the stock market. They control quality, cost, and risk. I believe in investing in the stock market, but you should have a conservative strategy and invest in low-to moderate-risk funds.

Real estate still has its risks. If you are in the real-estate game for a quick profit, then you might have the wrong investment. If you have the patience to wait three or four years (maybe longer) to make a real profit, then real estate is still a sound investment. Keep in mind that Mark and Kim are professional contractors. Before you go out and purchase a home for investment purposes, make sure you find good contractors that are capable of handling the renovations. If you don't have the money to go out and purchase a house, banks are still willing to give investment loans to qualified borrowers. Once again, the credit monster enters the room. Kim stated she has had great credit since she was 16. Good credit is very important. Make sure your credit is in good condition before you think about investing in real estate.

FROM NO COLLAR TO A WHITE COLLAR

Money in Giving Back

When you hear the strategy of holding on to wealth by giving back some of your earnings, it might seem like one big contradiction. How can you hold on to money when you are giving it back? On the other hand the Scripture states:

> Bring the whole tithe into the storehouse, that there may be food in my house. Test me in this, says the Lord Almighty, and see if I will not throw open the floodgates of heaven and pour out so much blessing that you will not have room enough for it.

(Malachi, 3:10, NIV)

This is the spiritual reference about the benefits of giving back, which I believe in following. When I give more to the Lord and His people, He blesses me beyond my imagination and what I thought was possible. I'm not in it for the financial gain but to be obedient and give back to my community. However, there are financial advantages associated with giving back to nonprofit and religious organizations.

The Internal Revenue Service (IRS) allows individuals to claim up to 50% of their adjusted-gross income (AGI) as donations to nonprofit organizations (IRS.gov).[14] Your AGI is the amount of your income that the IRS deems taxable. For example, let's say you made $200,000, and you gave $100,000 of it to nonprofit organizations. The IRS will allow you to receive a $100,000 credit towards your taxes. This means that you could end up with half of your income coming back to you from the government, and the taxes you would have ended up paying on the $100,000 goes into your pocket. For an illustration of the tax benefits associated with charitable giving, see the following table:

	Taxable Income without 50% going to charity	Taxable Income with 50% going to charity
Actual Income Earned	$200,000	$200,000
Donations to Charity	$0	$100,000
AGI	$200,000	$100,000
Tax %	30% ($60,000)	30% ($30,000)
Total Income after Taxes Paid	$140,000	$170,000

Table 2

Based on Table 2, with a 30% tax rate, you would get to keep an additional $30,000 of your income if you donated half of it to charity. You have been wondering all this time why philanthropists give away so much money. This is why. They are knowledgeable of the IRS tax codes and capitalize on the opportunities for holding on to wealth. The 50% rule applies to cash donations, and other types of donations are regulated by additional IRS tax codes. The example I gave was simple, but tax laws can get quite complicated. Make sure you seek the advice of a professional tax preparer when it comes to tax deductions. The IRS codes also state that any contributions in excess of $250 have to be documented by a legitimate nonprofit organization. If you do plan on giving back to charity, make sure the nonprofit organization is legal and that you receive a written receipt of your donation. To receive real benefits of giving back, you want to give from the heart and don't look for anything in return. Any monetary rewards you receive should be viewed as an acknowledgement of your support, not a payoff. Mark and Kim donate thousands of dollars each year to cancer foundations. I have never heard them brag one time about these donations, but I have been a witness to their generosity.

Risk Management

    After you have developed a plan for saving, investing, and holding on to wealth, you want to make sure you are prepared for the ceiling to cave in on your head. I am alluding to the fact that you have to be prepared for foreseen and unforeseen events. Multi-hustlers refer to this practice as risk management. According to Kim's theory, risk management consists of the following three actions:

1. Identifying risks
2. Reducing risks
3. Creating a contingency plan

If you are not prepared for events that could and will wipe out your wealth, then be prepared to lose everything you have worked so hard to get. The process is really simple. The first step is to write down every risk you can imagine that could jeopardize your six-figure income. Examine the events that a corporate hustler could encounter:

1. Loss of corporate customer
2. Loss of working hours
3. Reduction in pay
4. Increase in insurance

    The next step is to prioritize the likelihood and severity of each event. From the above list, it's obvious that loss of a corporate customer is highly likely and could halt your entire organization. The rest of the events were placed in order of likelihood and severity as well. After the events have been ranked, you want to reduce the risk of these events by avoiding them as much as possible. To reduce the risk of losing a corporate customer, try your best to meet or exceed the customer's expectations. This will reduce your chances of being laid off or terminated due to low productivity. Another way to reduce this risk is to find a corporate customer who has a history of stability. Many people try to obtain employment with the federal government due to its stability and benefits, such as the U.S. Postal Service. Even though the federal government has a history of being stable employment, it still functions as a corporate customer that could terminate your employment at anytime. Taking this into consideration, what happens when a foreseen event still occurs? That is when the implementation of a contingency plan becomes so important. A contingency plan is the same as a backup plan. In this case, multi-hustling is the backup plan. If a corporate customer terminates your services, you should have an independent hustle in place to make up for lost revenue. Once you have a contingency plan for the first event, you simply move on to the next one and repeat the steps. I have experienced every event named in the above list. In today's tough economy, a contingency plan should be a high priority.

Now let's examine the unforeseen events that an entrepreneur might encounter:

1. Loss of life
2. Disability
3. Natural Disaster
4. Lawsuit

These events can occur if you hold a corporate position as well, but they affect entrepreneurs on a larger scale. Loss of life is the inevitable that everyone chooses to ignore. When you die, someone has to take on the responsibility of handing your personal estate, such as the funeral service, unpaid bills, property, and legal actions. The only way that you can reduce this risk is to live a healthy lifestyle and pray that your time isn't near, but you still need a contingency plan in place. That is why it is so important to have life insurance. Life insurance is one of the reasons wealthy individuals are able to leave their families in good financial shape when they die. The family isn't left with an enormous debt, and they are able to carry on the wishes of the deceased. If you are an independent hustler and pass away, then you have an organization that is lost if you haven't prepared for this unforeseen event. The best thing for you to do is to have life insurance and a will, so your wishes can be carried out when you pass.

If you become disabled or experience a natural disaster, there are insurance policies that cover these events as well. In May 2010, Nashville, Tennessee experienced a "100-year flood" that devastated the city. As the name suggests, this type of flooding only happens every 100 years, but there were so many families and businesses that weren't prepared for this unforeseen event. Even if you live in the desert, you probably want to have flood insurance. A flood can occur anywhere on the planet, and you should not have a false sense of security that it couldn't happen to you. To combat the risk of a disability, stay in shape, buckle your seatbelt, and pray. That is the best advice that I can give you when it comes to a disability. Having good short- and long-term disability insurance would be your best contingency plan.

A wise man once told me that you will eventually get sued if you are in business long enough. You can reduce this risk by running your organization with the highest level of legal and ethical standards. The best contingency plan for a lawsuit is to retain a good lawyer. Even if you currently don't have any legal problems, a good attorney on standby can save you thousands of dollars in the long run. With today's access to pre-paid legal services, it's not as difficult as it once was to retain an attorney. If you do decide to purchase a pre-paid legal service, make sure you do your research. Some pre-paid legal services are worthless. Loss of a corporate customer, loss of life, and a lawsuit are just a few events that can ruin your hustle. Make sure you do the proper research for your industry and plan for any event that could occur.

As a multi-hustler you are depending on several sources of income to operate your organization. Keeping up with this income can be overwhelming, and income leaves your hands very quickly when you can't control it. You also have to incorporate operations and risk management in your activities. Kim's theory focuses on two simple formulas to manage these issues. The "10-20-70" formula focuses on dividing income into three parts: 10% giving, 20% savings, and 70% operations. This formula is used for an organization that is new and still needs the majority of its income for operations.

The "10-20-50" formula is for organizations that have gotten over the initial challenges associated with multi-hustling. This formula divides income into five parts: 10% giving, 20% savings, 10% investing, 10% risk management, and 50% operations. The percentages for giving, savings, and operations are self-explanatory, but what about investing and risk management? If you decide to purchase new equipment for your business or investment property, the 10% you have been saving for investing is where you find the funding for these purchases. You might not have saved enough money to pay cash for an investment property, but you should have enough money in your investment account to put a down payment on one. The money you set aside for risk management can be used to buy insurance to combat unforeseen events. When the formulas are used, there shouldn't be any event that you are not prepared to handle. Holding on to wealth can be very challenging, but now you have the tools that should make this task a lot easier.

10 WORDS INTO ACTION

After reading this book, you should be able to eliminate every excuse for not being successful. One of my primary goals was to focus on reality instead of wishful thinking or speculated success. Every subject and goal covered in this book was real, attainable, and plausible. Part I gave you the 10 keys of knowledge and the grand planning needed to immediately turn your situation around. Part II consisted of the case studies needed for you to conduct a good benchmark and study the practices of real multi-hustlers. Part III certified you to wear the white collar or the BDU of a boss. You have now obtained the equivalence of a master's degree in multi-hustling.

No one should be able to tell you that success is not possible, because you have an actual account of how to make dreams become reality. If I would have entertained the adversaries that surrounded me, I would still be working on page one of this book. The case study subjects and I have answered the call to become multi-hustlers, and now it's time for you to answer your calling. Mark had the tunnel vision to ignore the individuals laughing at him as he walked five miles to work everyday. He was an ex-convict. No one believed in him. Today, he is a millionaire. Who's laughing now? Glen didn't let one opportunity pass him by when it came to getting money. How many people do you know making $100,000 selling cable TV? Mignon disciplined herself to get up at 3:15 am, every morning, to hear the message God had for her. She is now on her way to opening up a second bakery to meet the demand of her customers. This is the same woman who fed her family of eight with $5. Do you think she is still feeding her family on a $5 budget? Kim was the daughter of a famous bank robber. She now manages one of the most successful construction companies in Tennessee. Instead of robbing the bank, Kim decided to break the bank. With her theory, do you think she can be stopped?

All of these individuals (including myself) became accustomed to hearing the word "no," but they never gave up on their God, their dreams, or themselves. Since you are now a certified multi-hustler, I leave you with the following charge:

> I charge you with never taking "no" for an answer. When others doubt you, make them out to be liars and accomplish everything they said you couldn't do. Exercise the 10 keys of knowledge and start your multi-hustle off in the right direction. Never be a part of negativity and always focus on staying positive. Realize the importance of grand planning and implement it in your hustle. Find a need in your environment and make plans to fulfill that need.

If creating a competitive advantage can make Fortune 500 companies billions of dollars, I know you can use the same concept to create a six-figure income. When I became successful at multi-hustling, I knew exactly how Melvin Williams felt when he said, "They dealt me a garbage hand. I turned it into a winner."[24] If society has dealt you a bad hand, get on your multi-hustle and turn it into a winning hand. Remember, the road to success will not be easy, but it will be well worth the journey. Go to war with your situation and become a battle-tested warrior.

After you have finished the last page of this book, begin your plans to better your situation and start a business. The only way you will ever be successful is by stepping out on faith and letting your intelligence do the rest. Release the chains of bondage and demand your freedom immediately. The only thing holding you back now is yourself. I want to be the first one to tell you, "congratulations!" You have gone from no collar to a white collar. Let the true executive in you shine. The time for talk has ended. It is now time for you to turn words into action.

ABOUT THE AUTHOR

Edgar Alan Cole is the owner and founder of two companies, E. Alan & Associates and One Team Publishing. Both of his companies were created from a small-business structure and promote ownership among team members and within his community. Before Edgar became an entrepreneur, he was a member of the U.S. Army for nine years. After serving honorably in the U.S. Army, Edgar decided to further his education by earning his bachelor's and master's degrees in business administration. The trials, tribulations, and successes Edgar has experienced in business are what motivated him to write this book. For Edgar, *From No Collar to a White Collar* is the blueprint for a grand plan to empower the disenfranchised. Email Edgar at eac502@yahoo.com to find out how you can get an autographed copy of this book.

RESOURCES

1. New World Encyclopedia. (2010). Creativity. Retrieved June 23, 2010, from http://www.newworldencyclopedia.org.

2. Dictionary. (2010) Reference. Retrieved June 25, 2010, from http://www.dictionary.com.

3. Linson, A. & Mann, M. (Producers), & Mann, M. (Writer/Director). (1999). *Heat* [Motion picture]. United States: Warner Bros., A Time Warner Entertainment Company.

4. Katzenbach, J. (1996). Real change leaders. *The McKinsey Quarterly, 4*(1), 148-163. Retrieved August 25, 2010, from EBSCOhost database.

5. YourDictionary. (2010). Faith definition. Retrieved July 22, 2010, from http://www.yourdictionary.com.

6. Pearce, J. and Robinson, R. (2004). *Strategic Management (9th ed.)*. New York: McGraw-Hill Companies.

7. The Franchise Mall. (2010). McDonald's. Retrieved August 15, 2010, from http://www.thefranchisemall.com.

8. Martinez, R. (2010) Transportation rates and services. *Multichannel Merchant, 6*(1). 37-38. Retrieved September 12, 2010, from Business Source Complete database.

9. Kerin, R., Berkowitz, E., Hartley, S., & Rudelius, W. (2003). *Marketing (7th ed.)*. New York: McGraw-Hill Companies.

10. White Pages. (2010). People search. Retrieved December 20, 2010, from http://www.whitepages.com.

11. Grimwade, N. (2009). Competitive advantage. *The Princeton Encyclopedia of the World* Vol. 1, pg. 208. 6pgs. Retrieved August 5, 2010, from ProQuest database.

12. Newmyer, B. & Silver, J. (Producers), Fuqua, A. (Director), & Ayer, D. (Writer). (2001). *Training Day* [Motion picture]. United States: Warner Bros. Pictures.

13. Jewell, E. (et al). (2001) *The Oxford American desk dictionary and thesaurus (2nd ed.)* New York: Oxford University Press, Inc.

14. Internal Revenue Service. (2010). Charities & non-profits. Retrieved October 11 2010, from http://www.irs.gov.

15. Business. (2010). The official business link to the U.S. Government. Retrieved October 15, 2010, from http://www.business.gov.

16. U.S. Small Business Association. (2010). Starting and managing a business. Retrieved October 15, 2010, from http://www.sba.gov.

17. Merriam-Webster Dictionary. (2010). Patron. Retrieved November 1, 2010, from http://www.merriam-webster.com.

18. Romans, C. (Reporter). (2010, October 11). *CNNMoney/Startups meet money* [Television broadcast]. Atlanta, New York and Washington, DC: CNN.

19. Kickstarter. (2010). A new way to fund & follow creativity. Retrieved October 11, 2010, from http://www.kickstarter.com.

20. Techstars. (2010). Funding. Retrieved October 11, 2010, from http://www.techstars.org.

21. Y Combinator. (2010). Retrieved October 11, 2010, from http://www.ycombinator.com.

22. Prosper. (2010). Retrieved October 11, 2010, from http://www.prosper.com.

23. Title Max. (2010). Retrieved October 11, 2010, from http://titlemax.biz.

24. BET. (2010). *Melvin Williams* [Television Series Episode] *American Gangster.* Retrieved November 20, 2010, from http://bet.com.

Made in the USA
Charleston, SC
11 July 2011